# Praise for *Chasing Wisdom*

"Some people write the book they aspire to live. Others live a book for years before they write it down. Daniel Grothe has been quietly living this book all his life, and I am so glad he has finally been persuaded to write it down. This book is fresh, countercultural, provocative, and urgent. I consider Daniel to be one of the truest pastors in America today, and this may well be one of his most important messages."

—Pete Greig, founder, 24/7 Prayer; lead pastor, Emmaus Rd Church; bestselling author, *Red Moon Rising*, *God on Mute*, and *Dirty Glory*

"For Daniel Grothe, this book is more than a life message; it is a passion embedded deep in his bones. A poet with his prose and a pastor who understands the care of souls, Daniel is the perfect guide in the critical quest for wisdom in our age. Let his stories and lessons learned be the medicine you so desperately need and the model for pursuing a sage."

—Glenn Packiam, associate senior pastor, New Life Church; author, *Secondhand Jesus*, *Discover the Mystery of Faith*, and *Lucky*

"As long as I've known Daniel Grothe, the driving force behind his life has been a desire for faithfulness, to walk the long road as best he can while taking as many of us with him as possible. His words will bring calm and correction. I firmly believe this message will save lives."

—Jon Egan, leader, Desperation Band; executive worship pastor, New Life Church

"I have had the privilege of sitting under the teaching and instruction of Daniel Grothe for years. He is a leader not only in the pulpit, but also in his community and home. Daniel is a man of his word and of the Word. He is one of the most powerful communicators of our generation. A book from Daniel is long overdue. I will read anything he writes."

—Esther Fleece, international speaker; founder and CEO, L&L Consulting; author, *No More Faking Fine*

"Daniel Grothe has a story we all need to hear. His life reflects an uncommon commitment to relationships that is both inspiring and challenging. This treatise will stir our imaginations and awaken us to a new love for the generations who have blazed the trails where we now walk."

—BRADY BOYD, SENIOR PASTOR, NEW LIFE CHURCH; SPEAKER; COHOST,
THE ESSENTIAL CHURCH PODCAST; AUTHOR, ADDICTED TO BUSY

"Daniel's book reflects the heart of a pastor who has faced some of the most difficult pastoral issues imaginable. He combines the desire for wisdom and a depth of love for people in a way that makes this book a compelling read."

—KEN COSTA, BANKER; PHILANTHROPIST; DEAN OF LEADERSHIP,
COLLEGE LONDON; CHAIRMAN, ALPHA INTERNATIONAL;
AUTHOR, GOD AT WORK AND STRANGE KINGDOM

"I've studied mentoring for years in my 30-year corporate career, and as a pastor's wife, speaker, and author. Daniel Grothe taps into what I've found to be a silver bullet of sorts, that of pursuing a chemistry with someone you want to do life with and stopping at nothing to make it happen. He tells us how and why this practice leads to a life more abundant. I started taking notes from the first few pages and will use this book as a resource for years to come."

—LYNETTE LEWIS, AUTHOR, CLIMBING THE LADDER IN STILETTOS;
WOMEN'S PASTOR, EVERY NATION NYC

"Throughout the Scriptures, we see the key role mentors and sages play in shaping the lives of men and women. Sadly, many in the church find our growth stunted, because we have not opened ourselves to this kind of formational relationship. I'm so grateful Daniel Grothe has laid out a fresh vision and an urgent need for us to search out and sit at the feet of wise guides. We need this book for the long-term health of our individual lives and local churches."

—RICH VILLODAS, SPEAKER; WRITER; LEAD PASTOR,
NEW LIFE FELLOWSHIP CHURCH, BROOKLYN, NY

"*Chasing Wisdom* is the book Daniel Grothe was born to write. His life is an ongoing testament to what happens when we refuse our society's idolatry of adolescence and embrace the kind of wisdom that can only come from those who have walked the path of faithfulness ahead of us. Buy this book. Savor it. And strive to live its message."

—ANDREW ARNDT, TEACHING PASTOR, NEW LIFE CHURCH;
SPEAKER; COHOST, *THE ESSENTIAL CHURCH* PODCAST

"In a world that idolizes heroes and high-profile celebrities, this book recognizes the need for people completely different: those who travel with us, full of truth and wisdom learned through long years of quiet faithfulness and obedience. Call them what you will—sage, confidante, trusted friend. Daniel shares powerfully his recognition of the need for such a person in his life. In following his journey, you cannot help but be prompted to address the question, Who is the sage in my life?"

—TIM HUGHES, PASTOR, GAS STREET CHURCH, BIRMINGHAM, ENGLAND;
WORLD-RENOWNED SONGWRITER, "HERE I AM TO WORSHIP,"
"SPIRIT BREAK OUT," AND "BEAUTIFUL ONE"

"There aren't many people under the age of sixty I would trust to talk about wisdom and sages. Daniel Grothe is one of the very few. I've had the privilege to record albums, lead worship, and hang out with Daniel, and he is exemplary, fun, and wise in all his interactions. He is wise beyond his years. I'm inspired by the way he follows Christ in his marriage, his family, and his ministry. Read this book over and over to build a solid foundation of wisdom in your own life."

—PAUL BALOCHE, WORSHIP LEADER; SONGWRITER, "OPEN THE EYES OF
MY HEART," "HOSANNA," "YOUR NAME," "OUR GOD SAVES," AND
"TODAY IS THE DAY"

# Chasing Wisdom

# Chasing Wisdom

The Lifelong
Pursuit of
Living Well

**Daniel
Grothe**

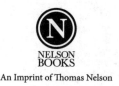

NELSON
BOOKS

An Imprint of Thomas Nelson

Published in Nashville, Tennessee, by Nelson Books, an imprint of Thomas Nelson. Nelson Books and Thomas Nelson are registered trademarks of HarperCollins Christian Publishing, Inc.

Published in association with The Bindery Agency, www.TheBinderyAgency.com.

Thomas Nelson titles may be purchased in bulk for educational, business, fund-raising, or sales promotional use. For information, please e-mail SpecialMarkets@ThomasNelson.com.

Unless otherwise noted, Scripture quotations are taken from the Holy Bible, New International Version®, NIV®. Copyright © 1973, 1978, 1984, 2011 by Biblica, Inc.® Used by permission of Zondervan. All rights reserved worldwide. www.Zondervan.com. The "NIV" and "New International Version" are trademarks registered in the United States Patent and Trademark Office by Biblica, Inc.®

Scripture quotations marked ESV are from the ESV® Bible (The Holy Bible, English Standard Version®). Copyright © 2001 by Crossway, a publishing ministry of Good News Publishers. Used by permission. All rights reserved.

Scripture quotations marked GNT are from the Good News Translation in Today's English Version—Second Edition. Copyright 1992 by American Bible Society. Used by permission.

Scripture quotations marked KJV are from the King James Version. Public domain.

Scripture quotations marked THE MESSAGE are from *The Message*. Copyright © by Eugene H. Peterson 1993, 1994, 1995, 1996, 2000, 2001, 2002. Used by permission of NavPress. All rights reserved. Represented by Tyndale House Publishers, Inc.

Scripture quotations marked NASB are from New American Standard Bible®. Copyright © 1960, 1962, 1963, 1968, 1971, 1972, 1973, 1975, 1977, 1995 by The Lockman Foundation. Used by permission. (www.Lockman.org)

Scripture quotations marked NKJV are from the New King James Version®. © 1982 by Thomas Nelson. Used by permission. All rights reserved.

Scripture quotations marked NLT are from the Holy Bible, New Living Translation. © 1996, 2004, 2007, 2013, 2015 by Tyndale House Foundation. Used by permission of Tyndale House Publishers, Inc., Carol Stream, Illinois 60188. All rights reserved.

Scripture quotations marked NRSV are from New Revised Standard Version Bible. Copyright © 1989 National Council of the Churches of Christ in the United States of America. Used by permission. All rights reserved.

ISBN 978-1-4002-1250-7 (eBook)

Library of Congress Cataloging-in-Publication Data

Names: Grothe, Daniel, 1982-author.
Title: Chasing wisdom: the lifelong pursuit of living well / Daniel Grothe.
Description: Nashville: Thomas Nelson, 2020.
Identifiers: LCCN 2019017149 (print) | ISBN 9781400212484 (hardcover)
Subjects: LCSH: Wisdom—Biblical teaching. | Well-being—Religious aspects—Christianity. | Christian life.
Classification: LCC BV4650 .G76 2020 (print) | LCC BV4650 (ebook) | DDC 248.4—dc23
LC record available at https://lccn.loc.gov/2019017149
LC ebook record available at https://lccn.loc.gov/2019980353

*Printed in the United States of America*

20 21 22 23  LSC  10 9 8 7 6 5 4 3 2 1

*For Eugene Hoiland Peterson (1932–2018)*

*Faithful Pastor*
*Timely Sage*
*Unexpected Friend*

# Contents

# INTRODUCTION

## Bullet Holes and Broken Hearts

*My tears have been my food*
*day and night,*
*while they say to me all the day long,*
*"Where is your God?"*

—Psalm 42:3 ESV

**S**ometimes our lives are sitting on top of a fault line without our even knowing it. Life can change in an instant. One such instant for me occurred on December 9, 2007.

On a quiet Sunday morning in Colorado Springs, a snowcapped Pikes Peak, known as America's Mountain, served as a beautiful backdrop for our church steeple. A fresh snow had fallen overnight, but we didn't let that keep us from gathering at New Life Church. A living legend, Dr. Jack Hayford, then in his seventies, was preaching that day. And best of all, God was with us. The song of the saints was joined with all the heavenly host, the Word of God was racing through the room with the Spirit's energy, and the children were running through the hallways. It was a beautiful day in the presence of the Lord. We had just finished our second morning service, and people were going to their cars with joy in their hearts and a bounce in their steps. Then, everything went horribly wrong.

Standing at the end of our church hallway, I heard what nobody ever expects to hear in church: rapid gunfire. I ran, darting into my pastor's office, shouting, "There's a gunman on campus!" In a fit of rage, a young man had stormed onto our campus with an assault rifle, a handgun, and a thousand rounds of ammunition, and sprayed bullets everywhere. He started shooting in our parking lot, attacking a family of six as they were getting into their minivan. Before racing into our church building, he shot through another car with a family of five in it. After entering the building, he continued his shooting spree. It was utter pandemonium. People were locking themselves in church offices and bathrooms and hiding in children's classrooms—and *everyone* was calling on the name of Jesus.

When the shooter was confronted by a security guard, he took his own life. His body lay in the hallway where, just two hours earlier, hundreds of parents were checking their small children into class. Rachel and Stephanie Works, eighteen and sixteen years old, died that day as Christian martyrs. Their father, David, was critically wounded and rushed into surgery. Everything about this was wrong. Some things should never happen. At church, you're supposed to kneel at the altar, not run for your life.

This senseless and violent attack on our church came only thirteen months after another great tragedy at New Life Church. On the morning of November 1, 2006, my boss walked into the lobby of the church, saw me, and came over. Normally a buoyant and bubbly guy, always the life of the party, he looked as if he were burdened with a thousand heartaches. Through muffled voice, he said, "This is going to be one of the hardest days in our church's history." He told me to walk with him, and as we moved through the building, he revealed that he had just received news about our senior pastor: a male escort had gone to several media outlets with the news that he was in a pay-for-sex-and-drugs relationship with our pastor. The escort had voice-mail evidence, making his allegations almost impossible to deny.

This news would have been heartbreaking enough on its own for any family and for any church, but our pastor happened to be the president of the National Association of Evangelicals (NAE), a group representing some thirty million American believers. Its headquarters was in Washington, DC, and many of us had made regular trips there to fulfill our responsibilities. When major debates swirled in Congress about same-sex marriage laws, major news agencies called our pastor for a statement. There were press conferences and private meetings with global leaders, such as Ariel Sharon, Israel's aging prime minister. Tom Brokaw and Barbara Walters brought camera crews to our church to report on what the community was doing. When Mel Gibson wanted to promote *The Passion of the Christ* to a large group of pastors, our church hosted. President George W. Bush even skyped into one of the pastors' conferences we were hosting, and our pastor—a Chevy truck driver—poked fun at the president's truck, a Ford.

The visibility of our pastor's role meant that this story would be the feature of every major news outlet. Up to this point, the attention we were getting had felt like success. It was all so *fun*. We were on top of the evangelical world, which I now recognize as a great irony, given that Jesus' vision of greatness had to do with washing dirty feet and carrying a blood-stained cross.

Now here we were, a church still reeling from the loss of our charismatic leader, in the middle of a senseless double murder/suicide on our campus. The scale of this tragedy was nothing short of Shakespearean. Our church that had been riding so high was now beginning a steep descent into the valley of the shadow of death. We were living Psalm 126 in reverse. After a long season of "shouts of joy," we were "sowing in tears" (ESV). For the next many months, we wept, we prayed, we mourned, and we braced ourselves for the road ahead. We gathered in homes to share meals and to comfort one another. We had corporate prayer meetings, searching our own hearts and repenting for the ways in which our "first love" had grown cold (Rev. 2:4 NJKV). A holy fear of the Lord began to return to a now contrite people.

## Life Is . . .

In her dazzling poem "The Summer Day," Mary Oliver asks a poignant question: "Tell me, what is it you plan to do with your one wild and precious life?"[1] We all know that life is precious, yes, and that there are moments of great serenity and gentle joy. We know the soft touch by the delicate hand of an aging grandmother, and we know the quiet glory of a sleeping newborn. The dew found blanketing the earth every morning, with absolutely no human effort, still amazes me and stirs my soul to praise. All I have to do is walk outside to find fresh mercy.

But for all its preciousness, life is also, at times, uncontrollably wild. Have you ever thought about how much a human being goes through on this pilgrimage around planet Earth? Life races along the route of the wildest roller coaster, heaving and thrusting, twisting and turning its way through all those dark tunnels of trauma. The sacred marriage that was once sealed in vows and meant to last a lifetime is ended with the stroke of a cheap pen purchased in bulk at Walmart. The children who were trained up in the way that they should go are now—like the prodigal son in Luke 15—sleepwalking their way through a far country while Dad sits on the porch weeping. The business venture that seemed so unsinkable, so *Titanic*, is taking on water.

Life is not colored neatly between the lines but is more like the confluence of two mighty rivers crashing together. The good creation that gives us groves of irrepressibly yellow aspen trees is the same creation that is sitting on top of fault lines that will soon shift and destabilize an entire region. The ecstatic celebration of a new birth is often followed by an unexpected funeral.

Much of the roller-coaster ride we experience is hidden, invisible to others but very much *felt* by those walking through it. The gift of mental health often degenerates into unhealth. For many, notable physiological mile markers, such as childbirth, menopause, and the steady yet sneakily sudden march into old age, are borne by wild chemical transitions that leave one feeling uncertain and unsettled.

As a pastor, I have a front-row seat to the unpredictability of the human experience. I show up at the hospital and catch the elevator up to the neonatal unit to visit the newest member of our congregation. The family and I celebrate, and while I hold the little baby girl, the parents tell me how much she weighed and how many inches long she was at birth. They recount the nerve-wracking, adrenaline-filled moments preceding the birth and the calm administered by the nurses after the storm of labor and delivery. We laugh as they reminisce, and I say something about the baby's pretty little nose looking just like her mommy's. I break open the anointing oil, quote a passage from Psalms, and thank God for this precious gift of life. I hug Mom and Dad, walk out of the room, grab a shot of hand sanitizer, and head to the elevators. But I'm not yet going to the parking lot. I now head downstairs to the oncology unit where another congregant is in the last stages of her fight with cancer. Within a span of thirty minutes, I have gone "up to the heavens" with those elated new parents and made "my bed in the depths" with a grieving spouse and children (Ps. 139:8).

Even as I was writing this last paragraph, a member of our congregation unexpectedly opened my office door, came in, sat down, and talked unabated for nearly fifteen minutes. She told me about her mother's most recent radiation treatment, which would be her last. Her mother's home has been made ready, and hospice care has been lined up. Her speech was grief speech. It was stream of consciousness, a meandering mind darting to and fro. It was exactly what I would have expected from someone in a fog, and it was just what she needed to keep going. I didn't say a word, except to pray at the end of our time. She just needed me to listen. We humans are constantly *transitioning*, bandying back and forth between the sharpest joys and the dullest sorrows.

Scores of people think they have a game plan, a coherent and thoughtful approach to life. But we all know that a plan doesn't mean anything when something goes horribly wrong. Or, as Mike Tyson once quipped, "Everyone has a plan until they get punched in the mouth."[2] There is a sort of epistemological certainty that can exist only for the young and untested. My wife, Lisa, and I probably unwittingly carried ourselves with that sort of overconfidence after having our first child. Lillian was sleeping through the night from the time she was six weeks old; she loved every vegetable we put in front of her, with broccoli being her professed favorite; she longed to read books; she never got sick; and she never tested the boundaries we put in place. We were tempted to think that so much of her easy demeanor was the result of our brilliant parenting techniques. But a child like that, while certainly dreamy, is setting up her parents for a rude awakening. Subsequent children who resist predictable sleep routines, refuse vegetables, and push the boundaries will quickly disabuse those parents of the notion of having the parenting thing nailed.

Life *moves* on us. Things shift, disruptions occur, and economies unexpectedly tank. The sturdy life we thought we had was, upon closer examination, more like a fragile house of cards than we would like to admit. If this is true, the question then becomes, *How do we become the kind of people who know how to handle whatever life throws at them?* How do we learn to think on our feet and navigate the terrain we never expected to traverse? In short—and this is the question at the bleeding heart of this book—how do we become *wise*?

## Wisdom Literature: Practicing for Spontaneity

The leaders and intelligentsia of ancient Israel allowed themselves to be occupied by these questions and gave the very best of their mental faculties to the effort of answering them. King Solomon got out his stylus and scroll, intent on engaging life's great enigmas. Four times he said, "I gave my heart" to know, to search, to observe (Eccl. 1:13, 17; 8:9, 16 KJV).

> I, the Teacher, was king over Israel in Jerusalem. I applied my mind to study and to explore by wisdom all that is done under the heavens. (Eccl. 1:12–13)

He also wrote,

> Get wisdom, get understanding: forget it not; neither decline from the words of my mouth. Forsake her not, and she shall preserve thee: love her, and she shall keep thee. Wisdom is the principal thing; therefore get wisdom: and with all thy getting get understanding. (Prov. 4:5–7 KJV)

The student of the Old Testament will discover that five books—nearly one-sixth of the Hebrew scriptures—are categorized under the genre known as *wisdom literature*. These books are Job, Proverbs, Ecclesiastes, Song of Songs, and some of the Psalms.

The book of *Job* is a painstaking account of a life that has fallen apart. But the story is thick with irony as the text describes Job as a righteous man. If we strictly read the Proverbs, we might be left with the impression that life runs *only* by a simple moral calculus; that is, a righteous person is *always* rewarded with a prosperous life, while the wicked suffer harm. However, the story of Job lets us know that things are not always so simple. The book of *Ecclesiastes* gives us a glimpse into the mind of a man who realizes life often doesn't work in the way we thought it would. The Bible, far from being a sanitized or oversimplified account of life in God's good world, is not afraid to name and address the troubling tensions we all experience on a daily basis. Solomon's *Song of Songs* stirs our passions, broadening the range of emotions appropriate to the human experience, letting us know the world can be experienced as a garden where the Lover and the beloved—God and his people—live in intimate harmony. The book of *Psalms* fits us for praise, giving us language adequate to our role as priests in the kingdom of God. And the book of *Proverbs*, when read with the long view in mind—with the *eschaton* in mind—brings us full circle. When God finally makes all things new, the righteous will flourish and look in triumph on their foes.

These five books make up Israel's wisdom literature. They show us the complexity of the human experience, and function for the believer a bit like how musical scales function for a jazz musician. I got my first set of drums when I was two years old, and I've been playing my whole life. Through the years, I've played in several jazz quartets. In a good quartet, the upright bassist and the drummer hold down the rhythm section, usually with a pianist; and to round out the group, a saxophonist, guitarist, or trumpeter will usually step to the front to play all the lead melodic lines and feature on most of the solos. Think John Coltrane on tenor sax. All great jazz musicians have at least three things in common: (1) they have gone into the practice room and learned and internalized all the scales, which are simply organized sequences of notes, until they can play them forward and backward; (2) they have put in the time to learn all the standard jazz songs (in jazz parlance, they've "learned the book"); and (3) they can play every one of those standards in any key.

"Oh, you want me to play Duke Ellington's 'Take the A Train' in C?" No problem!

"How 'bout we play 'A Night in Tunisia' in D?" You got it.

"Hey, man, you good with playing Brubeck's 'Take Five' in E-flat minor?" Sure thing.

If these three things are in place—knowing *all the scales* and *all the songs* in *any key*—a great jazz musician can walk into any club, on any night, in any city, and be ready to play. Living a life of wisdom is a lot like becoming a great jazz soloist. As counterintuitive as it may seem, we have to practice for spontaneity. We have to do our homework ahead of time, so we're able to creatively improvise when the moment arises. A life of wisdom is about learning to think on our feet, about learning to be responsive to the actual conditions of life.

It's time for many of us, like the jazz musician, to get back into the practice room—to get out the Scriptures and put ourselves before the all-wise God; to take all that we're reading into the place of prayer; and to ask the eternal Sage, whose endless wisdom is available to all, for clarity on all the perplexing dimensions of our lives. The practice room gets us ready to improvise on the stage we call life, which is so precious and so wild.

## Into the Practice Room

The following pages of this book are an invitation into the practice room. Once inside, you will be introduced to skilled instructors who can show you the way, those who can apprentice you into the art of living well. For practice rooms are not primarily meant for the individual, but rather for the community. This book will be an overview of a few of the great saints of the Christian tradition, and to one sage in particular who has meant so much to me: Pastor Eugene Peterson.

In each chapter, I will discuss a crucial practice, a necessary discipline that I believe must be found in any life that can properly be called wise. And with each practice, I will share a story of what I learned throughout my ten-year friendship with Mr. Peterson. So right here at the start, as you're looking to understand how this book is organized, feel free to get settled into that flow: *practice* and *story*. Prepare to learn from the saints of old and the sage himself, Mr. Peterson, on this quest into a life of wisdom.

# ONE

# Learning to Ask for Help

"Ask and it will be given to you."

—Jesus of Nazareth (Matt. 7:7)

I n his bestselling book *Outliers: The Story of Success*, Malcolm Gladwell gives us a glimpse of several major players on the world stage. He covers tech industry leaders like Steve Jobs and Bill Gates, and music industry pioneers like The Beatles. Gladwell is interested in what fueled their astronomical ascendancy. How did they break through? Many are quick to assume that these people are on the scene because they are "the best and brightest" of their generation, possessing an intellect and talent so prodigious and a work ethic so irrepressible that they were simply *destined* to make it. Certainly, they are smart, hardworking, and brimming with creativity, but Gladwell comes to the conclusion that their success is also largely attributable to their access to help—and their willingness to ask for it.

## Nurturing Holy Presumption

In 1994, in a rare interview, Steve Jobs sat down with the Silicon Valley Historical Association. The conversation had Jobs musing about the life of the entrepreneur and the risks and failures that are intrinsic to one lived challenging the status quo. In passing, he told a story that is instructive for anyone who knows there's still room to grow. Jobs was a young, inquisitive, prepubescent kid, living in the basin of the tech industry's fertile valley named *Silicon* when he heard about a legendary figure residing across town: Mr. Bill Hewlett, cofounder of the Hewlett-Packard Company. The story he told next baffles the mind:

> I called up Bill Hewlett when I was twelve years old and he lived in Palo Alto. His number was still in the phone book! And he answered the phone himself. "Yes?" I said, "Hi, I'm Steve Jobs, I'm twelve years old; I'm a

student in high school and I want to build a frequency counter."[1]

While other twelve-year-olds that day were at the city library, or wandering their neighborhood streets, or skateboarding in the grocery store parking lot, this twelve-year-old kid was on the phone with the leader of one of the greatest companies on the planet. Talk about *chutzpah*. Young Jobs had more moxie than most people thrice his age. He had done his homework and was prepared for the call, intent on not squandering the opportunity. After describing his introduction to Hewlett on the phone, Jobs went on:

> "I was wondering if you have any spare parts I could have?" And he laughed. He gave me the spare parts for the frequency counter, and he gave me a job that summer at Hewlett-Packard working on the assembly line putting nuts and bolts together on frequency counters. He got me a job at a place that built them, and I was in heaven.[2]

Jobs finished the story with a profound and surprising observation:

> I've never found anybody that didn't want to help me if I asked them for help. . . . And I've never found anyone

who said no or hung up the phone when I called. I just *asked*. And when people ask me, I try to be as responsive and pay that debt of gratitude back. Most people never pick up the phone and call, most people never ask, and that's what separates sometimes the people that do things from the people that just dream about them. You've got to act![3] (emphasis mine)

As I reflect on the people I want to be like, I see a common thread: they walk with a sort of holy presumption. It is not an unhealthy presumptuousness that they carry themselves with, not a narcissistic impulse to look out for *number one*, but an awareness that there are resources available if they just know where to look and are willing to ask. They have developed muscle memory in asking for help. They pick up the phone and call. They knock on the closed door and expect that on the other side of it will be someone congenial, someone willing to let them in. They are the people who find it easy to trust the words spoken by Jesus in his most iconic sermon: "*Ask* and it will be given to you; *seek* and you will find; *knock* and the door will be opened to you" (Matt. 7:7, emphasis mine).

Indeed, it seems to me that many people are withering away because they are too polite. This form of politeness is often rooted in not wanting to be a burden to others. We don't want to interrupt someone else's life, don't want to get in the way of people who are surely too busy. At other points, we are simply unwilling to do the hard work of engaging what we know will be a difficult, soul-searching process. In pastoral counseling sessions, I tell people all the time that "it's going to hurt either way." There will be pain that comes from putting in the effort, or the pain that is the result of continuing to ignore something that needs attention. "The danger," writes acclaimed journalist Alina Tugend, "is that stalling can let the situation grow from a problem into a crisis."[4] So we might as well choose the route of running *into* the pain and have something to show for it.

## Help Is All Around

Given life's unpredictability and the inevitability of pain and hardship, what do we do when that pain and hardship show up on our doorsteps? In roughly AD 270, there was a man in Lower Egypt named Antony. He was born into wealth and had everything going for him. He had access to a great education and two loving parents who owned three hundred acres of productive fruit trees. In a region of the world that was difficult to tame because of the climate, his parents were self-sustaining, and Antony had the security of a great inheritance awaiting him some day. But when he was around eighteen years old, one of those life crises swept in on the young man: both of his parents died. He was now alone and heartbroken. Mercifully, financial security was not going to be a problem for him, though money could not replace the love of his parents. One Sabbath day, Antony, a God-fearing man, was going up to the Lord's house and found himself reflecting on the early Christians. He was pondering how many of them sold their possessions and gave the proceeds to the poor. As he walked into the temple, the priest was beginning his homily, and the gospel reading that day happened to be about Jesus talking to the rich man: "If you want to be perfect, go, sell your possessions and give to the poor, and you will have treasure in heaven. Then come, follow me" (Matt. 19:21). Antony, cut to the heart by Jesus' words, left the temple that day, arranged for the sale of his land, and distributed the money among the town's poor. He then headed for the desert.

We now know him as Saint Antony, one of the desert fathers, one of those John the Baptist–like cave-dwelling figures who gave himself over to the ascetic life. Sainthood, though, is often misunderstood. We think of it as an exercise in rugged individuality, a Lone Ranger's attempt at holiness. Being newly orphaned and having given away his possessions, Antony was the perfect candidate to strike out on his own, but he modeled a different kind of sainthood. A biography written by one of his apprentices says,

If he heard of a good man anywhere, like the prudent bee he went forth and sought him, nor turned back to his own place until he had seen him; and he returned, having got from the good man as it were supplies for his journey in the way of virtue. . . . He subjected himself in sincerity to the good men whom he visited and learned thoroughly where each surpassed him in zeal and discipline. He observed the graciousness of one and the unceasing prayer of another. He took knowledge of one's freedom from anger and another's loving-kindness; he gave heed to one as he watched, to another as he studied. One he admired for his endurance, another for his fasting and sleeping on the ground; the meekness of one and the long-suffering of another he watched with care, while he took note of the piety towards Christ and the mutual love which animated all. Thus filled, he returned to his own place of discipline, and henceforth would strive to unite the qualities of each and was eager to show in himself the virtues of all.[5]

Saint Antony's story is one of finding wisdom and help in the rubble, in the heartbreaking loneliness of an orphan's life, and of finding these gifts *even in the desert*. But his acquisition of wisdom wasn't simply the result of some private, mystical dispensation from the heavenlies. He had read the stories of the queen of Sheba traveling a great distance "to test Solomon with hard questions" (1 Kings 10:1). He knew what King Solomon had said: "Wisdom is the principal thing; therefore *get wisdom*" (Prov. 4:7 NKJV, emphasis mine).

Wisdom is found in seeking God; wisdom is acquired in face-to-face encounters with the sages. Remember what was said about Antony? "If he heard of a good man anywhere, like the prudent bee he went forth and sought him." And remember what happened? "He returned, having got from the good man as it were supplies for his journey in the way of virtue." The result of his search for wisdom among the sages was remarkable, and wisdom was a gift that kept on giving. In his old age, a young man sought him out in the desert and became his apprentice. The apprentice's name? Athanasius. Yes, Saint Athanasius, the one who would become the church's great defender of the faith, of *orthodoxy*; one who would help draft the Nicene Creed and embolden the church to stay tethered to the truth in the storm of heresy and deception. Athanasius would never have become *Saint* Athanasius without submitting his life to Saint Antony, the sage. And Saint Antony became a sage only after years of apprenticing himself to the wise ones around him. This is how any wise person comes into being.

So many of us know what it is like to find ourselves in the desert of grief and loss, of sin and shame. But we've been tricked into thinking that the desert has to be a place of barrenness, that life has to stay stuck, and that we have to go it alone until we get things together and can resettle our lives back in the city where there's security. The truth is, though, that help is all around. The desert can blossom, and life can be lush in the most unlikely places. Doxology leaks from the prophet Isaiah as he shouts the good news:

> Instead of the thornbush will grow the juniper, and instead of briers the myrtle will grow. This will be for the LORD's renown, for an everlasting sign, that will endure forever. (Isa. 55:13)

Throughout church history, we discover communities of wisdom that kept God's people from crumbling in crisis: monks and mystics, spiritual directors and seers, hermits and nuns, the desert fathers and mothers. These are communities of sages, and the sages are still living among us.

## Survival of the Weakest

Our world is drunk on power. "Only the Strong Survive" was Jerry Butler's hit song in 1968, and we haven't forgotten it since. Philosopher and sociologist Herbert Spencer, after reading Charles Darwin's *On the Origin of Species*, coined the phrase "survival of the fittest."[6] We then took the phrase and ran with it. Plenty of little boys grew up hearing their fathers tell them that real men don't cry.

"But why, Dad?"

"Because it's *weak*, boy. Don't you know that it's a dog-eat-dog world out there?"

In the shadow of the Roman Empire, the world's most dominant kingdom at the time, a young Jewish itinerant preacher sprang up. This man was bouncing around the region proclaiming a truer and more enduring kingdom than the Romans would ever know—the kingdom of his Father. But when darkness fell each evening on this man who had so much authority, the foxes and the birds had it better than he did; at least they had a predictable place to lay their heads (Matt. 8:20). This poor man didn't want anyone's pity, however, because, though he possessed nothing that could be written into a will, he possessed something no one could take from him: an identity, *sonship*. This, not a home or possessions, was true security. And what was this man's message?

"The meek . . . shall inherit the earth." (Matt. 5:5 ESV)

The eternal Word of God put his feet down on solid ground and proclaimed to the world that a special place had been carved out in his Father's heart for the meek and the weak, for those poor in spirit and in pocketbook, and for those whose bellies growl for food and for righteousness. He said that the real war—the war in heavenly places—is won by the merciful and the peaceful. For all the low-life losers on the fringes of Roman power, this was truly good news.

If you live, as I do, in a Western, first-world country, you are more like the ancient Romans than you could ever know. Most of us can travel, are well fed, have relatively secure governments with military might that provide a sense of security. Many of us have health care readily available, and can communicate with almost anyone in the world at the drop of a hat. For many of us, life is *working*, or at least it might seem so to the casual observer. And when it's not working, we lie through our teeth and insist that it is. Our standard greeting of "How are you doing?" is met with a predictable response: "Great!"

I grew up within a Christian subculture where it was common for people, when asked how life was going, to respond reflexively with something like "blessed and highly favored." Such response was based not so much on how life was *actually* going, but on how we *wanted* it to go. The thought was that if we're going to have it go well, we have to first speak it into existence. I understand where that comes from. I'm okay with having a positive outlook on life, and with carefully choosing our words. But when holding a faith position comes at the cost of being truthful, when it keeps us from being able to acknowledge when things are actually quite terrible at the moment, we have crossed over into dangerous territory.

I'm not totally sure why we feel the need to fake it, to hide behind the "I'm doing just fine" façade. We are either so used to having our needs met that we don't know how to ask for help, or we are so scared of acknowledging that our needs aren't being met that we keep quiet. We think, *What will people think of me?* We tell ourselves we ought to be able to figure this out, and we think it's a sign of weakness to ask for help. But isn't that precisely where Jesus' proclamation comes in? His announcement was a declaration of the survival of the *weakest*, a statement that only those *who know they need help* and *who are willing to ask for it* can be saved.

> "Ask and it *will* be given to you." (Matt. 7:7, emphasis mine)

## Chasing Eugene

When I was a young pastor and our church went through a horrific stretch of tragedy and trauma, I was very aware of just how quickly things could disintegrate. It was a season of existential threat. At times, I was like one of those faithless disciples hyperventilating in the back of the boat, unsure if we would make it through the storm, and pretty convinced that Jesus was somewhere napping while we were all going down. But it was just then that I came across one of the sages who would save my life. His name is Eugene Peterson, and his book *The Contemplative Pastor* washed ashore in my life like a message in a bottle. I found this book while standing in a brightly lit Goodwill store. I read it in a day and knew that it contained just what I needed.

My parents had taught me to ask for help, had helped me to acquire a holy presumption. So I sat down and wrote Eugene a letter. Since I didn't have contact information for him, I sent the letter to his publisher with a short cover letter asking them if they could pass it on for me. I walked out of my front door to the mailbox, my feet clapping against the sidewalk, my hands carrying the letter to a perfect stranger, and my heart gently holding the possibility that this letter, sent out into a cold and impersonal world, could end up in the cosmic shredder. But before its composition, I had asked myself, *What's the worst that can happen?* In my mind, the worst-case scenario was being ignored; or the next, and only slightly more dignifying step up the rejection ladder, was a polite no. I had made my peace with either scenario. Regardless of what happened, I would be able to thank God for

Eugene's work in writing *The Contemplative Pastor*, and I would be able to thank Eugene. The letter was now out of my hands.

A few weeks later, I came home from work and went to the mailbox just like I did every other day. But this day was different, because *there it was*: a white envelope with my name handwritten in distinctive cursive. (I have it sitting on the table in front of me as I type this.) You know, the cursive a grandparent uses because they were educated in a different era when they cared about such things. *That* cursive.

When I looked in the top left corner of the envelope, I saw:

E Peterson
Lakeside, Montana

Time stopped. You've got to be kidding me! I opened it and read the first line:

Dear Daniel,
    Yes, I would be willing to spend a day with you here in Montana.

He said *yes!* And that day a fresh measure of courage rose up in me, making me believe I could weather the storm.

Over the years, I've come to think of asking for help as a sign of great maturity. Many of us feel alone and are lonely. Many of us have big decisions to make and don't know what to do. Many of us are in the middle of a desert season and feel like the heat is going to overwhelm us. But there are people out there. People like Bill Hewlett. People like Saint Antony. People like Eugene Peterson. People who are ready to help us in our need. We only have to be willing to ask. But *will we?*

You have nothing to lose and much to gain, so keep your eyes open. Seek out someone with a convincing and beautiful life and ask for help.

# TWO

## Introducing the Sages

For though you might have ten thousand *instructors*
in Christ, yet you do not have many *fathers*.

—Saint Paul of Tarsus

(1 Cor. 4:15 NKJV, emphasis mine)

**G**reat-grandma Cora was born in 1889, and it was
1996 when she was asked the question. Her great-
grandson, Jason, was given an assignment at school: find
someone who has lived a long time and ask them, "What
was the greatest time of your life?" Cora was 107 years
old, so she had plenty of decades from which to share.

Was it the Roaring Twenties? The Fabulous Fifties? The Yuppie Eighties?

Without hesitation, she said, "The greatest time of my life was the Great Depression."

"Well . . . um . . . [clears throat] . . . *excuse me?*"

"The greatest time of my life was the Great Depression, because of the simplicity, community, and joy."

In essence, great-grandma Cora was saying that the Great Depression caused her family and community to live how God intended his creatures to live: with unbreakable bonds of fidelity to one another. They *needed* each other—not abstractly, but concretely—every day.

While she never attended seminary, great-grandma Cora was a front-porch theologian. They are the people who sit on their front porches and study the way the world works. They pay attention to people, have a feel for the neighborhood, and watch life unfold. The Old Testament loosely refers to them as *sages*, and every ancient Near Eastern society had them. A sage on the front porch can peer down the street and, seeing a father berating his son, predict that if he keeps it up he will have a rebellious teenager a decade from now. Another sage, sitting in the town square and watching a shady businessman deal ruthlessly with his vendors, can say with absolute certainty that in the long run it will not go well with that man.

Whoever walks in integrity walks securely, but whoever takes crooked paths will be found out. (Prov. 10:9)

Sages are people who have learned how to live. They are composed and have mastered the fundamentals. Like great-grandma Cora, they have strung together decades of holiness and carry themselves with dignity. They radiate a kind of strength that causes others to rise. They are wholesome, their lives are worth emulating, and when they speak, people listen because they have something to say.

In our information age, we would be wise to remember Saint Paul's words to the Corinthian believers that we will never be short on teachers. He assured the Corinthians that they would have an overabundance of people who want to advise and instruct them (1 Cor. 4:15). At the risk of sounding flippant, I'd say Paul didn't know the half of it. He could never have imagined the content factory our society would become—the podcasts and YouTube channels, the surfeit of blog posts and sixty-second Instagram sermonettes.

But after Paul gave his assurance, he pivoted. He continued that while there may be many instructors, there will be very few who would be able to parent us, to direct us, to embody what a beautiful life of faithfulness looks like. We have a shortage of true spiritual moms out there. We don't have enough dads to show us the way.

Paul wasn't saying anything new. As noted earlier in the introduction, in the Old Testament we find five books known as Israel's wisdom literature: Job, Proverbs, Ecclesiastes, Song of Songs, and some of the Psalms. But what exactly are they *for*? These books were meant to guide us squarely into the possession of wisdom, to surround our lives like scaffolding as God builds in us a life that will never crumble. These wisdom books are sturdy pillars to keep the community of faith from collapsing.

> Wisdom has built her house; she has set up its seven *pillars*.
>
> (Prov. 9:1, emphasis mine)

> By wisdom a house is *built*,
>     and through understanding it is *established*;
> through knowledge its rooms are *filled*
>     with *rare* and beautiful *treasures*.
>
> (Prov. 24:3–4, emphasis mine)

We have all heard the same warning: it takes decades to build a beautiful life and ten seconds to tear it down. Israel's wisdom literature was written so that the "simple" (Prov. 1:4) would be instructed and, thus, saved from a life of "woe" and "sorrow" (Prov. 23:29). But these books were not just do-it-yourself manuals for the ancient

Israelites to take home and study. The people of God were given these flesh-and-blood sages, these spiritual guides who lived right down the street from them and could show them the way.

Most of us don't know much about the sages because it is so much easier to know about Israel's superstars (the prophets) and superintendents (the priests). I don't classify them like this because *they* thought of themselves this way, but rather based on the priority *we* give them and their writings today.

We like the prophets because they were stalwart figures who were larger than life and so *certain* about their call to repentance. There's not a lot of wiggle room in their proclamations; they're pretty cut-and-dried. The prophets heard from God and spoke to the nation.

"Repent!"

"Wake up!"

"Come, let us return to the LORD!"

The prophetic shouts startled and awakened a people careening toward a cliff. The prophetic ministry was necessarily a ministry of austerity because the prophets embodied the pathos of a God who, in his furious love, refused to abandon his people to their own rebellion. God, through his prophets, just kept coming at his people. The prophets were often dramatic, sometimes becoming illustrations of their own sermons. Think of Isaiah going naked and barefoot for three years (Isa. 20:1–3). *This is what will happen to God's enemies!* Think of Ezekiel lying in the dust for 430 days (Ezek. 4:1–6). Think of John the Baptist in the desert with clothing made out of camel's hair, living on a strict diet of locusts and wild honey (Matt. 3:4). Even if people didn't always heed their call, the prophets were unmistakable.

Then there were the priests, the ones who regularly summoned the people of God into the house of God. While the prophets flew high at 35,000 feet, the priests were *on the ground* with the people. The priestly task was to keep Israel's social identity and ritual practices intact—calling the people to prayer, fasting, worshiping, and bowing down before Yahweh; making sacrifices on behalf of the people; and collecting tithes and offerings to be distributed to the poor living among them. The priests took the prophetic oracle and worked to help the people live it out.

Prophets and priests. One spoke to the nation, the other to the synagogue. But what about the sages? Who *are* they? What do they *do*? And why do we so desperately need to rediscover them today?

Sages have been trained over the course of decades by the spiritual discipline of trial and error. They have lived and practiced their craft and gained insights along the way. Although they have not done everything right over the years, they have figured out how to stay within the safe boundaries of Lady Wisdom's instructions (see chapters 1–9 of Proverbs) and, as a result, have built a life that honors God. In every ancient Near Eastern society, they would have been at the city gates—at the confluence of commerce and politics—adjudicating disputes between family members and business partners. After listening to all parties involved and weighing the facts, they would have given a fair ruling. These sages weren't peripheral to civil society; they made civil society possible. And they can be found everywhere in the Bible.

## Sages in Scripture

Think about Jacob who became Israel. On his deathbed he called for his twelve sons, who later became known as the twelve tribes of Israel. With power and precision, he spoke about and into their futures. Scripture tells us that in his dying moments, "Jacob called for his sons and said: 'Gather around so I can tell you what will happen to you in days to come'" (Gen. 49:1–2). And then he blessed them and sent them out into their futures. *That's the touch of a sage.*

Think about Moses' brilliant father-in-law Jethro, swinging into town for a visit, only to discover that his son-in-law, the newly established leader of the nation of

Israel, was about to die of exhaustion because he was a foolish workaholic. Jethro's advice cured him and saved his life (Ex. 18). *The touch of a sage.*

And, of course, we have the power couple, Priscilla and Aquila (Acts 18). They were from Rome, but sometime during the reign of the emperor Claudius (AD 49), they, along with the rest of the Roman Jews, were expelled from their homeland. The minority Jews, a peaceful people, were somehow seen as a threat to the world's greatest empire. Priscilla and Aquila found themselves settling down in Corinth (Greece), and it was there that they bumped into Paul, former Pharisee previously known as Saul. They would have known who Paul was, because in the not-too-distant past, he was complicit in the murder of Stephen, the first Christian martyr. Luke tells us in Acts 7:58 that they "dragged [Stephen] out of the city and began to stone him. Meanwhile, the witnesses laid their coats *at the feet of a young man named Saul*" (emphasis mine). And Saul was just getting started. Acts 8:3 tells us that "[Saul] began to destroy the church. Going from house to house, he dragged off both men and women and put them in prison."

Understandably, Paul had a soiled reputation among Christ-followers. So what did Priscilla and Aquila do when they bumped into this character? They took him in, treated him like family, and gave their lives to him. These people who had no home became a home for Paul. They spent eighteen months in Corinth discipling him, teaching him how to live, and helping him get all that old ungodly ambition and anger out of his system. There's a beautiful detail found in Acts 18:18 that we shouldn't miss:

> Paul stayed on in Corinth for some time. Then he left the brothers and sisters and sailed for Syria, *accompanied by Priscilla and Aquila*. (emphasis mine)

Behind every great historical figure, one can find at least a small circle of close friends who helped them carry their assignment through completion. Which is exactly what I think this couple did for Paul. Indeed, he took them along because he *needed* them—their significant strength, their unwavering support, their friendship, and their wisdom. *The touch of a sage*.

## The Near Invisibility of a Sage

A few years ago, my wife and I bought a home that needed some repair. We purchased it from the people who built it more than forty years earlier. They were in their early eighties and had no desire or energy to update it. It was *their* place, and they loved it the way it was. We appreciated the history of it, and we were sure that the bones of the house were solid, but we were less emotionally attached and wanted to make some changes right away. The green shag carpet and the orange paint on the walls had to go. So, over the last couple of years, we have completed several house projects. Friends and family who had seen it when we first bought it would notice the changes, and might say something like, "I just love the way you painted the fireplace!" Or, "The new floors look nice." But you know what no one has ever said? Nobody has ever come into our house and said, "Wow, I just love your load-bearing walls! I just love how they keep the place from collapsing. They're so essential." It's always the *cosmetic* stuff that gets their attention. But it's the *infrastructural* stuff that makes a home possible.

Sages are like the load-bearing walls. They are the infrastructure that God gives us to keep our lives sturdy. A sage can save your life, but sometimes they can be hard to spot. Most of the time they are nearly invisible because they blend right in. In 1631, the great Dutch painter Rembrandt brilliantly demonstrated this reality in his painting called *Simeon's Song of Praise*, which is a depiction of Mary and Joseph bringing the eight-day-old Jesus to the temple.

The old man Simeon was there, where he always was, thinking about and yearning for what he always thought about and yearned for: the salvation of God's people.

When the little baby showed up in the temple, something happened in Simeon. He was *moved*, and the moving was "by the Holy Spirit," as Luke tells us three times in three verses (Luke 2:25, 26, 27). Luke says that "Simeon *took* the child in his arms" (v. 28 GNT, emphasis mine). Notice he does not say that the parents *gave* the child to Simeon. So here's the scene: an old man praising God and shouting while snatching up an eight-day-old baby from his parents, because in this child he had *seen* something.

Six times in four short verses we are told that, in the Spirit, Simeon perceived something: "[He had been] *looking forward* to the consolation of Israel" (v. 25 NRSV, emphasis mine in all four verses); "It had been *revealed* to him by the Holy Spirit that he would not *see* death before he had *seen* the Lord's Messiah" (v. 26 NRSV); "*Guided by* the Spirit, Simeon came into the temple" (v. 27 NRSV); "For my eyes have *seen* your salvation" (v. 30 NRSV). Finally, he blessed the young family and prophetically declared the vocation of Jesus and the plight of the holy family.

I have studied many paintings of Simeon, and here's what stands out to me: you can only see half of his face in most of the paintings. Rembrandt's depiction of Simeon, while entitled *Simeon's Song of Praise*, scarcely seems to be about Simeon. In the painting, the Christ-child's face is gleaming, which one would expect, and the glory of God is all around him. Mary is in awe as she kneels before the altar steps, and light is beaming down on her as she holds one hand over her womb and the other over her heart. Joseph is next to Mary, characteristically tucked away in the shadows, staring at the child with eyes full of questions.

And then there is Simeon, the subject of Rembrandt's painting. He's in the middle of the action, holding the baby in his arms and his face shining brightly. But something about this painting is strange: you can see only the *side* of Simeon's face. You can't see his eyes as he looks up to the heavens. If the painting is as the title says, if the song is truly Simeon's, then why isn't he the focal point?

If Rembrandt's painting has anything to teach us, it is that you will only catch the sideways glance of a sage. Sages always have the obscured faces in the crowd, and their pictures are often tucked in the back of the family's photo albums. They're the invisible characters, or maybe it's more accurate to say that they are translucent, always allowing the light to pass through them because—like Jacob, like Jethro, like Priscilla and Aquila—they exist for one thing: to build up and secure someone else.

## The Particular Crisis We Face

If we are not careful, we will squander the gift God has for us: the community of wisdom *that will save our lives.*

We have been trained to pay attention to the young and the beautiful, to the pop stars and the athletes, but will we notice the sages who are quietly and unobtrusively standing by with what we need? There is wisdom available to us, but unlike ancient times when the sages were woven into the fabric of a community, a sage today must be purposely identified and thoughtfully pursued.

My mind wanders back to Simeon in the temple. What happened after everyone went home that day? Did they see him in a new light? Did anyone hear Simeon's wisdom and think, *I need to pursue him and his depths of wisdom*? Did anyone invite him over for dinner to glean from his years of deep fellowship with the Holy Spirit? Did anyone *see* Simeon and discover in him the sage they needed?

Saint James, the half brother of Jesus, reminds us, "If any of you lacks wisdom, you should ask God, who gives generously to all without finding fault, and it will be given to you" (James 1:5). Wisdom is available to us. The sages are living among us.

But what should we be looking for? Look for people who are joyful and composed; those who are living lives of "robust sanity."[1] Look for people who have a simple joy radiating from their eyes. Look for people who have been faithful—faithful in work, faithful to their friends, faithful in marriage. Look for people who have wholesome, stable relationships, instead of a trail of relational debris cluttering the landscape of their lives. Look for people who, as long as their health allows, tend to stay physically active and vibrant. Look for people who have learned to steward whatever finances have been entrusted to them; those who don't live excessively or ostentatiously (though some of them will have plenty of money), but instead live simply, generously, and appropriately. The sages seem to know what is fitting for the moment, and they live openheartedly before the Lord and openhandedly with people.

I'm sure there are sages right around you if you'll keep your eyes open. But it's going to take some work to pursue them. Will you do what it takes to seek them out? I can promise that if you do, you will be glad you did.

# THREE

# Learning to Work for Wisdom

*Above all and before all, do this: Get Wisdom!*
    *Write this at the top of your list: Get*
    *Understanding!*
*Throw your arms around her—believe me, you*
*won't regret it;*
    *never let her go—she'll make your life*
    *glorious.*
*She'll garland your life with grace,*
    *she'll festoon your days with beauty.*
        —Proverbs 4:5–9 THE MESSAGE

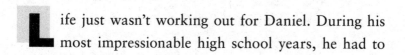

ife just wasn't working out for Daniel. During his most impressionable high school years, he had to move away from his New Jersey home to the big city of Los Angeles. He already felt uprooted and lonely enough, being so far from his friends, when the most ruthless of his classmates sensed his melancholy and, like sharks trailing blood in the water, came swarming in for the kill. Johnny, the self-appointed big man on campus, might as well have been the offspring of that Philistine named Goliath. Johnny became the face of Daniel's misery, and one Halloween night, he and a mob of teenage boys, drunk on testosterone, pounced on Daniel, beating him senseless. Haymaker punches were landing right and left when out of nowhere an old man—*wait, isn't that the janitor?*—jumped in and unexpectedly manhandled the crazed mob. His name? Mr. Miyagi.

After the fight, Miyagi carried Daniel to his house, cleaned him up, then sent him home. But their partnership was only just beginning. The pressure from the bullies was going to keep coming for Daniel, so Mr. Miyagi, a master martial arts instructor, agrees to train him to withstand the onslaught. Johnny was a skilled martial artist in his own right, and so to stop the bullying, Daniel, a novice, would have to beat him on his own turf. The early morning training sessions commenced, and strict rules were set in place. Mr. Miyagi would not settle for anything less than Daniel's excellence. And you know the rest of the story: after a rigorous period of training, and against all odds, Daniel-san beats Johnny in the championship fight. But, more importantly, in the process of becoming a good fighter, Daniel becomes an even better man.

Though this isn't a true story, *The Karate Kid* won countless awards in 1984, and the movie still stands the test of time. Why? I think the enduring appeal of the tale of Mr. Miyagi and Daniel-san can be attributed to the fact that we know in our bones that the acquisition of a meaningful life will require every bit of focus and every shred of energy we have. Because Daniel was a novice fighter, there was so much to learn, and when he got frustrated with the process and tried to cut corners, Mr. Miyagi sternly rebuked him with these words: "First learn stand, then learn fly. Nature's rule, Daniel-san, not mine." There are no shortcuts along the way to a life of maturity. You can't skip steps and still end up with a sturdy life.

*The Karate Kid* is an introduction to the shape and substance of Christian discipleship. One of the more poignant interactions is found in the early days of their training, when Mr. Miyagi says, "We make sacred pact: I promise teach karate to you, you promise learn. I say, you do, no questions." The master *teaches*, the disciple *learns*. This is a story that reinforces what any lifelong student of wisdom already knows: anything worthwhile is worth working for.

## "Yes . . . But Not So Fast"

When I first encountered Eugene Peterson's work, I desperately needed it. I was the young Daniel-san, locked in a fight that would determine whether or not the practice of my pastoral vocation would endure. Out of nowhere, Master Eugene jumped in and, with utter precision, fought off my enemies. The help came in the form of his book *The Contemplative Pastor*. That book picked me up and brushed me off. It stood me up on my feet again as a young pastor. I was being trained and, in the process, made more fit for the task. To say thank-you, I decided to write Eugene that first letter. In the letter I requested a day of his time to talk things through.

As I mentioned before, when I wrote him, I honestly expected my letter to go unanswered. But to my surprise, he said yes! I was stunned. His opening line read, "Dear Daniel, Yes, I would be willing to spend a day with you here in Montana." My deep gasp sucked all the air out of the room, but I quickly filled it back up a moment later with my outrageous laughter. *Eugene Peterson wrote me back and said I could come see him!* I could have dropped the letter on the kitchen floor and danced the dance of a thousand jubilees. But I'm glad I didn't because, though he had me on the hook, his very next sentence was about to jerk all the slack out of my line: "But not so fast."

Even as I type this, I can feel the tension I felt when I first read that line. *But not so fast.* It was as if a song had taken an unexpected turn into a minor-key musical interlude when it seemed like it was only going to be majorly happy. His letter went on with a tone that was not only *not* conciliatory, but was construed by many of my friends as quite brusque and uncongenial. Here's the full text of his first letter:

Dear Daniel,

Yes, I would be willing to spend a day with you here in Montana. But not so fast. I think it would be better if you spent some time thinking about what is involved. Why don't you take some time to reflect on what "pastor" exactly means to you. And what "church" means to you. Write a couple of pages on each, pastor and church, and send them to me.

The reason? I don't want you to waste your time with me. You have spent your life in huge churches that are about the furthest thing from being church that I can think of. And your work as a pastor has been in settings (willingly?) that virtually make it impossible to be a pastor. I doubt very much that you could get anything out of a day's conversation with me by trying to fit it into the church you have been chosen to be in and the pastor you have been hired to be.

You say you have read a lot of what I have written. So you must know that there is nothing glamorous about the church as I understand it. And that there is little adrenaline in the vocation of pastor as I have practiced it. I don't think churches are glamorous. And I don't think pastors run on adrenaline.

You have been a practicing part of the Americanization of the church that I think has been degrading if not outright destroying both the church and the pastoral vocation. Do you think there is enough common ground to even begin a conversation?

If you think there is, I will be happy to welcome you. I just don't want it to be a touristy visit.

> The peace of our Lord,
>
> Eugene

You can see why I might have felt the tension. What I would learn about and from Eugene in the decade to follow would soften and clarify his views on the life of a pastor in a large church,[1] but his initial letter was an announcement, a reckoning, a gauntlet being thrown down to see if I was ready to rise up. Indeed, if it's true that anything worthwhile is worth working for, then a good sage must also know the value of an apprentice's hard work. If Eugene had been too gentle with me in our initial correspondence—if he had given me a cheap yes that had me racing right out to his home for a quick visit—he would have been setting me up for failure. I have come to think of his "but not so fast" as four of the most important words to ever be directed my way. And what followed next from Eugene indicated that he was not at all going to be in a hurry.

The first letter I sent Eugene was dropped in the mail on November 15, 2008, and I was shocked when he responded on December 8. I took a few weeks to write my papers on "pastor" and "church" as he requested, and finally sent them his way. He responded with another letter, saying that he liked my papers, that we indeed had enough common ground to begin a conversation, and that he would be happy to host me. In that letter he gave me his phone number. "Give me a call and we'll set up your first trip." It took us about two months to get to this point.

One day, I received a call from a phone number I didn't recognize. I was giving a drum lesson at the time, so I ignored it, letting it go to voice mail. After the lesson was over, I listened to the message and, to my shock, it was Mr. Eugene Hoiland Peterson *himself.* Missing a call from a legend felt so wrong, like missing a call from the Oval Office. Eugene's voice was low and gravelly, sounding something like a small boat engine gurgling under the water. It was the sound of old age, mixed with deep introversion. Old, retired scholars like Eugene spend the lion's share of their time thinking, reading, and writing in their studies, so when they *do* speak, their voices, like old classic cars, take some time to warm up. "Hi Daniel, Eugene Peterson here. Give me a call when you can."

Adrenaline shot through my system, and I nervously walked around my basement trying to prepare for what I would say when I called him back. I did my best to compose myself, tried to act like this was just another phone call, and slowed my breathing down. I dialed his number, starting with Montana's 406 area code. *Here we go.* It rang . . . and rang again. Those rings had eternity in them. And then there he was: "Hello, this is Eugene."

I introduced myself, and he warmly thanked me for my letters. This was the call where we were going to settle on a date for my visit, and I was like a kid at Christmas. I had my laptop out, ready to purchase my flight as soon as he gave me the date. But on that call, he told me that some things had changed. He wasn't going to be able to meet with me right away like he'd said. He had just turned in his manuscript for *Practice Resurrection* (on Ephesians), his fifth book in five years, and he was tired. "Jan and I are going to take a nine-month sabbatical. I still very much look forward to getting together, but it's going to have to wait." He asked me to call him in nine months, and we would get it scheduled.

Now, I might have been tempted to think something like:

*Come on, Eugene! Don't you know I'm hurting? I just told you that our church lost our senior pastor to a moral failure. And did you forget that we had a madman storm into our church parking lot with an automatic rifle and a thousand rounds of ammunition, killing two precious teenage girls before committing suicide in the hallway of our children's ministry? Don't you remember that? Don't you remember I'm young and need some help? You can't make an exception to meet with me right away?*

But by the sheer mercy of God, I didn't think that. In those following nine months, I kept buying and reading more of his books. Whenever Eugene quoted other brilliant thinkers, theologians, poets, and pastors in his books, I would snatch up *their* books and familiarize myself with their work.

I finally showed up at his front door on April 6, 2010, exactly 507 days after I had written my first letter. Sure, Eugene was tired after writing five books in five years, but looking back, I also think he was vetting me. I think he was waiting to see how much I *wanted* to meet him, to see if I would stick it out. The way Eugene made me work for it ended up lighting a spark in me that became a roaring flame of desire to grow, to read, and to pursue wisdom. In those 507 days, I can count nearly thirty books that I bought and read that Eugene introduced to me through his own writing. Moreover, during that time, I enrolled in Fuller Theological Seminary and spent the next seven years pursuing my master's degree in theology.

When Eugene wrote his "but not so fast" letter, I think he was channeling his inner Jesus. Think of Jesus, blazing with holiness, walking up to those young, untrained, and surely unfit-for-the-task disciples and saying to them, "Whoever wants to be my disciple must deny themselves and take up their cross daily and follow me" (Luke 9:23). He shoots them straight. How badly do you want it, ladies and gentlemen? While I don't believe he was intentionally trying to run people off by making the Way unnecessarily difficult, I also don't think keeping everyone happy was his top priority either. Jesus knew they could do it, knew they could rise up into a life humming with holiness. But he also knew that it would cost them everything—that all their backup plans would have to be taken out back and given a decent burial, and that every false and idolatrous version of the good life they had would have to be stripped away from them.

Being apprenticed to Jesus for seventy-five years had prepared Eugene for making an apprentice out of me. He had learned that walking in the way of wisdom rarely comes easily, and so, like a good sage, he made me work for it. A true sage knows how to lead an apprentice on a journey that will make more of them by the end of it.

## Disturb Us, O Lord

We live in a society that prizes intellectual safety and security. We so much want our universities to be "safe spaces" for students that many professors, who have devoted their lives to particular disciplines, no longer feel as if they are allowed to challenge their students. The moment a student feels unsettled or feels as though one of their beliefs is being wrongfully called out by a professor, the very real threat of a lawsuit looms. Never mind that universities have historically been the precise place where students are sent to be challenged, to have their misguided views disturbed. Today, we are living in a "culture of safetyism"[2] that is stunting many American minds and keeping us from having many of the conversations we need to have.

The franchise players on professional sports teams are pandered to and have more power than the coaches and general managers. (Bill Belichick notwithstanding!) If a superstar decides to throw a fit, and the owner has to choose between the franchise player and the coach, it's likely that the coach will be cleaning out his office on Monday morning. We are living in a cultural milieu that's allergic to a Miyagi-like arrangement of discipline and strict apprenticeship. And as long as that's our status quo, we all but guarantee our perpetual adolescence.

But Christians come from a long line of people willing to be chastened and challenged. Consider this prayer:

> *Disturb us, O Lord, when*
> *We are too pleased with ourselves,*
> *When our dreams have come true*
> *Because we dreamed too little,*
> *When we arrived safely*
> *Because we sailed too close to the shore.*
> *Disturb us, O Lord, when*
> *With the abundance of things we possess*
> *We have lost our thirst*
> *For the waters of life;*
> *Having fallen in love with life,*
> *We have ceased to dream of eternity*
> *And in our efforts to build a new earth,*
> *We have allowed our vision*
> *Of the new Heaven to dim.*
> *Disturb us, O Lord, to dare more boldly,*
> *To venture on wilder seas*
> *Where storms will show Your mastery;*
> *Where losing sight of land,*
> *We shall find the stars.*[3]

Disturb us, O Lord! Have your way. "Not my will, but yours be done" (Luke 22:42).

In a world that prizes safety and security at all costs, many Christians are willing to be disturbed, are willing to be unsettled, are willing to work for it.

## Welcome to Discipleship 101

The word *apprentice* means "a person who is learning a trade or art by experience under a skilled worker."[4] It comes from the Latin word *apprehendere*, which means "someone who apprehends." It doesn't mean someone who apprehends *easily*, or who just picks it up *right away*, but someone who refuses to leave the side of the master, who refuses to stop when things get difficult; in other words, someone who is actively learning along the way.

And isn't this exactly what Jesus had in mind when he called that motley crew of folks to follow him, to become his disciples? The Greek word for "disciple" is *mathētēs*, which simply means "learner." And learning takes time—and error. All of Jesus' disciples messed up and embarrassed themselves. James and John wanted to destroy a city by calling down fire on it (Luke 9:51–56). Peter was quick to assure Jesus that he'd never deny him (Matt. 26:35), but we all know what happened only a few hours later (vv. 69–75). On and on it goes, their stories of imperfections, coming to a full crescendo in Judas's betrayal and their wholesale scattering on that very dark Good Friday night. But for all their issues, eleven out of the twelve showed back up when Jesus rose. They came out of hiding and got back on track. By the power of the Holy Spirit, they became true disciples. They worked for it, they learned, they threw away all their backup plans. They took up their crosses and followed Jesus. And, in the process, they changed the world. This is Discipleship 101.

When I'm doing it right, I'm submitting myself to wise people who know Jesus, and who will call me to a life of cross-shaped obedience. People who will challenge me and give me books to read. People who will ask me the hard questions and push back when they think I'm telling only half the story. People who, like Eugene Peterson, will kick my butt and help shape up my spiritual conditioning.

How about you? Are you willing to work for it? Do you have any of those Miyagi-like figures in your life? If so, have you invited them to challenge you into a deeper engagement with wisdom? Because anything worthwhile is worth working for.

# FOUR

# The Wisdom of Loving Scripture

*Oh, how I love your law!*
*I meditate on it all day long.*
*Your commands are always with me*
*and make me wiser than my enemies.*
—Psalm 119:97–98

**W**isdom is not to be confused with our present-day fascination with positive tips and life hacks and five-step strategies for learning how to navigate life more successfully. Wisdom is not some amorphous concept floating "out there" in the ether, or some quiet state of mind that knows how to shut out those pesky cries of the world around us. Wisdom is more specific. King Solomon, who spent his life trying to chase wisdom, put it this way so very long ago: "*The fear of the LORD is the beginning of wisdom*" (Prov. 9:10, emphasis mine). Wisdom, says the New Testament, is found as we worship—and *only* as we worship—Jesus, the Word of God made flesh.

Saint Paul himself, who had spent the formative years of his life looking for and yet missing out on wisdom, was stopped dead in his tracks one day by Christ the Lord. Paul first had to be blinded to everything he previously knew before he could see the truth. And what he saw was *Jesus*. In his letter to the Colossian believers, Paul called Jesus "the mystery of God . . . in whom are hidden all the treasures of wisdom and knowledge" (Col. 2:2–3). All of this can be summed up in this simple little axiom: The degree to which we give ourselves over to Jesus is the degree to which we will find ourselves growing in wisdom. But how exactly do we give our lives over to Jesus? How do we fall in love with Wisdom himself?

## The Only Book We Have

For Lisa and me, one of the most magical experiences of parenthood has been watching our three kids acquire facility with the English language. Our strategy in the early years of their development was simple: read as many books to them as we could. Early on, I'd stand among them at bedtime like a street performer in New York City and read *We're Going on a Bear Hunt* with all the verve I could muster. Their hearts raced faster as my voice grew louder, and they were utterly transfixed. On quieter nights, as their eyelids gently flickered, Lisa would read to them from *The Giving Tree* or *Charlotte's Web*. When they were young, they took in the language primarily through their *ears*. When they turned two and had learned to sing their ABCs, we got them their own little alphabet-tracing books, with which they began singing and sketching and scribbling their way into this new linguistic world. This next phase of language acquisition was marked by getting the language into their *mouths* and into their *hands*.

I think we learn the language of faith in much the same way. As Paul wrote in his letter to the Romans, "So then faith cometh by *hearing*, and hearing by *the word of God*" (Rom. 10:17 KJV, emphasis mine). As we hear the words of the Bible trumpeting forth—words like, "Love your enemies" (Matt. 5:44) and "Bless those who curse you" (Luke 6:28)—the smoldering embers of our lukewarm lives are stoked into a blazing beauty. We get up early in the morning and, with the psalmist, rehearse what's true: "His love endures forever" (Ps. 136). We give ourselves over to the words of this Book and somehow know that the ruins of our lives are being rebuilt by the Master Craftsman. We, like little children, *hear* these words, *write* down these words, and *take* up these words on our lips. Yes, for the Christians, the Bible is our book, and we believe that in it all truth is to be found. As in Psalm 1:2, we are to "meditate" on these words, and as we do, our faith grows, wisdom deepens, and love expands. We cannot rehearse this story of the God who raised Jesus from the dead too much.

Some of you may be thinking, *But why are Christians so insistent that the Bible is the book? There are a lot of great books out there.* Let me take a minute and tell you why Christians, through the ages, have believed the Bible to be our book.

## Scripture as *Sacrament*

Since the time the ancient scrolls were passed down to us, Jews and Christians have read the sacred Scriptures *sacramentally.* That word may be new to many of you, so let's take a minute here to work this out together. Exactly what is a *sacrament*, and what does it mean to read the Scriptures *sacramentally*?

First, a sacrament is a divinely appointed conduit of

God's grace, a container that carries the glory of God. Think water baptism or holy communion. Although you can find God elsewhere, the church has said that, more often than not, the sacraments are *the place* where you will most regularly find God. Of course, you can experience the majesty of God when you're on a mountain hike. Of course, you can be caught off guard with "the beauty of his holiness" as you're reading poetry. Of course, you can be made aware of God's love in a fresh way as you hold your firstborn child. Of course! But, as the church has insisted for over two thousand years, there are certain *moments* and certain *means* of grace that will be disproportionately filled with the glory and the majesty, the wisdom and the wonder of God. More than when you're on a mountain hike and more than when you're reading a moving poem, you will find God's glory in his church, among his people, in the receiving of his sacraments.

But sacraments can be tricky because they look so *ordinary*. The two most common sacraments in the church—holy communion and baptism—are made up of the most common materials of human life: bread, wine, and water. This is an awareness that ought to fill us with great joy, namely, that God insists on infusing the ordinary stuff of our lives with his glory; or, we could say it this way: a sacrament is grace hiding in plain sight. There is a reordering of what we have come to understand as ordinary. The objects right in front of us, the stuff of our daily lives, become *more*. God takes the materials of human existence and repurposes them so that his boundless life comes racing through to the believers as they, by faith, give themselves over to the seeming absurdity of the act. As believers approach the altar with empty hands and open hearts, by the power of the Holy Spirit, the broken bread becomes a participation in the body of Christ that takes our brokenness and lifts it up into his wholeness. And in the cup, we find the restoration of covenant, the removal of alienation, and the return of joy.

*Bread?* The crumbs that humans in every corner of the globe have eaten since the beginning of time? You mean to tell me that the simple flour mixed with water and baked over fire can be a genuine encounter with the living Lord Jesus? The church has said *yes*, ever since Jesus passed the bread to his friends on the eve of his death.

And consider the sacrament of baptism. Since the time John the Baptist dunked Jesus into the Jordan River, the church has insisted that the waters of baptism are a unique place of encounter with Jesus. This may sound ridiculous to many of you. *Water?* You mean the stuff we drink and use to wash dishes and do laundry? The stuff that falls from the sky and makes the crops grow? *That* is a conduit of God's grace, a means of receiving his mercy? Yes. That is what the church has proclaimed for over two thousand years. The same water that makes crops grow can, in baptism—by the work of the Holy Spirit and the faith of the believer—make our lives grow. Marilynne Robinson put it best in her Pulitzer Prize–winning novel *Gilead*: "It is easy to believe in such moments that water was made primarily for blessing, and only secondarily for growing vegetables or doing the wash."[1]

A sacrament is proof of God's unbounded creativity. And the sacraments are a special place for God to meet us!

So, what does it mean that Christians read the Scriptures *sacramentally*? Aren't the words on the page just words? In his book *Scripture as Real Presence*, Hans Boersma shows that the early church fathers understood the Bible to be a place of special encounter with Jesus. In the mid-second century, Clement of Alexandria wrote, "They that are ready to spend their time in the best things will not give over seeking for truth until they have found the demonstration from the Scriptures themselves."[2] In the fourth century, Saint Athanasius (300–375) wrote, "The Holy Scriptures, given by inspiration of God, are of themselves sufficient toward the discovery of truth."[3] In another letter, he wrote, "The Catholic Christians will neither speak nor endure to hear anything in religion that is a stranger to Scripture; it being an evil heart of immodesty to speak those things which are not written."[4] The

Bible was *the book* for the church fathers, so why would we try to go elsewhere to find truth today?

Could God give us a special encounter with Jesus as we read *Sports Illustrated* or the newspaper? Sure. Could he awaken us to his glory as we read through the phone book? Of course. "Our God is in heaven; he does whatever pleases him" (Ps. 115:3). But for some reason, more often than not, God the Son is most likely to meet us as we open the Bible. The words on these pages somehow become *more* than just words. By the power of the Spirit, they pulse with the life of God and bring us face-to-face with Jesus. And as we continually put ourselves in front of these words, with an attitude of openness and humility, God mysteriously acts upon us, transforming our motivations and attitudes, purifying our affections, and drawing us into himself. For over two thousand years, the church has asked, "Do you want to find God? Well, we'll tell you where he can be found. Keep opening the Book." The Bible is the place where Jesus can be encountered most often.

## Eugene Peterson: The Sage Who Loved Scripture

When I found Eugene Peterson's *The Contemplative Pastor* on the shelf of a secondhand bookstore ten years ago, I recognized his name. I thought, *Hey, isn't that the guy who translated* The Message *Bible?* At the time, I didn't know he had written other books. I discovered later just how prolific a writer he was and bought every book he had ever written (some thirty-five books, as I count them on my shelf). But when I got to know the man, I realized just how much the Bible had formed every bit of his life. He was a kid who grew up in a Pentecostal church in a small town in Montana. His parents took him to church every time the doors opened. He was a kid who was exposed to all the fiery preachers who passed through town. Their sermons stirred in him a wildly vibrant biblical imagination. So vivid was his biblical imagination that he would get on his bike and ride into the Rocky Mountains to pretend he was David, the young shepherd boy. David killed lions and bears; Eugene killed deer and elk.

Eugene told me the story of the summer when, as a teenager, he memorized Psalm 108. The end of the psalm is David's impassioned verbal assault against Edom, Israel's enemy.

> Have you not rejected us, O God?
>> You do not go out, O God, with our armies.
> O grant us help against the foe,
>> for human help is worthless.

With God we shall do valiantly;

   it is he who will tread down our foes.

(vv. 11–13 NRSV)

He told me how he would pace the streets of Kalispell at night with Psalm 108 on his lips when he got angry.

After getting his undergraduate degree in philosophy and English at Seattle Pacific University, Eugene packed up his car and moved to New York to study at the New York Theological Seminary, and later at Johns Hopkins University in Baltimore. This was a man who was learning to devote his life to the Book. Through the years, he demonstrated a mastery of the biblical languages— Hebrew, Aramaic, and Greek—and was hired by the New York Theological Seminary as professor of languages.

When I was with Eugene in the mornings at his home, we would sit quietly in his study. I remember one morning watching him from across the room. He sat in his rocking chair with his worn-out Bible in his lap. Occasionally, he would reach over and grab his coffee mug. Sometimes he would run his fingers through his rugged gray beard. For over an hour, not a word was spoken. It was one of those few experiences of a silence so true that it becomes almost distractingly loud. But Eugene was right at home; I realized that *I* was the problem and quickly settled in. Eugene was doing what he had spent his entire life doing:

giving his unhurried time and undivided attention to the words of life.

And the lifetime investment he made in the Scriptures was obvious. When he prayed, the Scriptures poured out of him. When he talked, he used biblical metaphors and sharp scriptural allusions. When he wrote, it was like reading one of the poets of ancient Israel, because their words had so permeated his imagination. Reading Eugene's work is like stepping through the wardrobe into a new world.

When *The Message* translation came on the scene and sold some sixteen million copies, people were amazed. Many wondered who this Eugene Peterson was. Eugene, meanwhile, was stunned by the response it received. A reserved and introspective man, he was also caught off guard by the attention he was given. Why? Because *The Message* wasn't some sort of external achievement. It was the thing Eugene's whole life had been about. It was the thing that almost inevitably had to spring from his life. Out of the abundance of his heart, Eugene's fingers typed.

I'm not saying all this as a way of listing Eugene's accomplishments. He was thankful for and satisfied with the work he had done, of course, but he wasn't much impressed with himself and regularly grew weary of the acclaim. He lived with a holy indifference to it all. I mention his lifelong love for the Scriptures not as the *end point,* but as a *setup* for the thing that matters most: Eugene Peterson lived a beautiful and faithful life.

To be with Eugene was to know that you were in the presence of a holy man. There was an invigorating wholesomeness, an overwhelming purity, that you encountered when you were in his presence. His eyes were clean. His smile was an almost overwhelming explosion of joy. His heart was tender. He lived out the human vocation of bearing the image of God into the world. I'm not trying to divinize him. During his eighty-five years, I'm sure his life bottomed out at times. But by the end, he had come to be a saint in the truest sense of the word. How did that happen? It happened because Eugene Peterson lived his life face-to-face with Jesus through a living and daily encounter with his Word.

## Falling Back in Love with Our Book

We see it happen every day. People are seeking and searching and yearning to find the next wave of wisdom. People are anxious to discover the secret key that'll unlock the door to a life that matters. Yet many of them are missing out on the gift that's right in front of their faces, the Book that's collecting dust on the coffee table. Do you want to find wisdom? Do you want to steep your life in the truth? Do you want to know who God is? What he had in mind for his good world, and what he intended when he created humans in his image? Hide your face in the Book. And what is the result of hiding our faces in the Book, of reading the Bible sacramentally? As you do, the wisdom that has been promised will begin to find its way in.

After years of reading the Scriptures and endeavoring to *obey* them, we become like the jazz musician who can improvise flawlessly because she learned all the scales. We can step into any situation and discern what is right and good, what is fitting and appropriate. Internalizing the Scriptures makes it so that we can play any song in any key. By spending years meditating on Proverbs 5–7, we become able to quickly identify cheap seductions and destructive situations *before* we get trapped in them. After years of reading the Sermon on the Mount sacramentally, as a place where God can be found, we find ourselves freed up from the anger that rots our bones, and more practiced in blessing those who curse us (Matt. 5–7, particularly 5:38–48). Falling in love with the treasury of Scriptures makes us "wiser than [our] enemies" (Ps. 119:98) and those who are trying to chart their own way. And while all of this may not happen quickly, if we stick with it—if we allow the Bible to be our book—it will happen.

But how do we do it? Are there routines we can follow? In Psalm 119, Israel's longest and maybe most iconic psalm, we read,

I rise before dawn and cry for help; *I wait for Your words*. (Ps. 119:147 NASB, emphasis mine)

The Hebrew verb *yachal*, which means "to wait," has a figurative image behind it: a lioness waiting, tarrying, scanning the horizon for, say, a gazelle to come into view. As the hunt is developing and a potential kill is coming into sight, the lioness is the paragon of poise. She is totally focused and completely still. She takes pains to ensure that the moment is not squandered. In this moment only one thing matters. The psalmist said he "waits for" God's Word like that. But how many of us do the same?

The psalmist also rises "before dawn" to open the Scriptures and *wait*. It's the first thing he does, and from it, everything else flows. But some of us hate early mornings, or find them difficult because we are tending to young children at night or working the late shift. That's fine. There's plenty of flexibility in the life of faith. Life is dynamic and seasonal, so there's no need to feel as though *early* is the only way. The people of God had other psalms that might suit your situation better:

My soul waits for the Lord more than the watchmen for the morning. (Ps. 130:6 NASB)

This psalm shows someone waiting for the Lord through the dark watches of the night. Sometimes it takes everything and everyone quieting down for us to be ready to hear from and speak honestly to the Lord. The gates of the kingdom are never shut, and we serve a God who "neither slumbers nor sleeps" (Ps. 121:3–4). Take an hour of your night. Turn off your phone or put it in a drawer, then open the Scriptures and read. Learn the discipline of pushing through the distractions and the seemingly endless supply of fleeting thoughts, and let the words of God wash over your life. Read the Bible aloud so you can hear it, which is what so many of the saints who have gone before us recommended. And read slowly. There is no prize at the end for the fastest reader. Keep a journal nearby and highlight the words and phrases that stand out to you, then turn these words into prayer.

Perhaps it works better for you to steal away for fifteen minutes on your lunch break to read, or listen to the Scriptures while running on the treadmill. In any case, let the words awaken your heart and transform your imagination. Experience the Scriptures as a daily sacrament, as a container of God's grace, and as a channel through which his glory washes ashore in your life.

Trust the psalmists. Let the words of holy Scripture make you wise.

FIVE

# The Wisdom of
# Going to Church

As for the saints in the land, they are the
excellent ones, in whom is all my delight.

—King David (Ps. 16:3 ESV)

I n peacetime—that is, when things are going well—too
many of us live like fools. When our bills are being
paid on time and the children are relatively healthy, when
work feels like it's clipping along and all we can see in the
future is a bright horizon, we should be thankful. But we

should also beware. These are the moments when it's easy to get sloppy. We begin to befriend the status quo. We take the path of least resistance. We take the low road simply because it requires less from us. And as much as we hate unimaginative clichés like the ones I've just used, we look up one day to discover that we've actually been *living* one. Sadly, sometimes only a crisis can wake us up.

As a pastor, I see this every day. I spend an inordinate amount of my life with people, in their highest highs and their deepest lows. I celebrate weddings and grieve the unexpected divorces; I officiate baptisms and preside over burials; and I dedicate young babies to God and pray with parents waiting for their twentysomething prodigal to come home. My work often situates me on the frontlines of the human condition.

If I were to diagnose the greatest threat that comes against believers in peacetime, it would be twofold: *boredom* and *distraction*. We grow weary of doing the same old things we have done for, say, the last two decades. We feel like we have "been there, done that" with all this Jesus stuff, and wonder if this is all there is. Our boredom causes us to forsake the routines that were a part of our holy formation. We put down the Bible. We stop going to church. We get distracted and turn away from the disciplines that got us where we are to see if there's something new and flashy out there. Like the believers in the church of Ephesus, many of us have left our "first love" and "have fallen" away from the things we "did at first" (Rev. 2:4–5 NASB). The fire of our love for Jesus "that once burned bright and clean"[1] has turned into a pile of flickering embers.

I have observed this church-abandoning phenomenon particularly among those who are in the middle of life, between the ages of forty-five and fifty-five. When we are younger, we are just humble enough to acknowledge that we need help. Life seems so complex. We are looking for decent work and a stable living situation, hoping to get our feet squarely under us. The need for support is especially acute for young couples raising small children. We watch the news and realize just how high the stakes are in this crazy world. We somehow instinctually know that the old "it takes a village" axiom is right; so we're more willing to get the kids up, get them fed and dressed, and drive them to church. Indeed, the latest Pew Research poll bears out my theory.[2] And according to *Christianity Today*, "about 2 out of 3 American adults who regularly attend church or other religious services say they go *for their kids*" (emphasis mine).[3]

When we grow older and the simplest tasks become more difficult, when we are faced with the reality that our bodies are failing and so many of our friends are dying, there is no denying that we need help. The church, when functioning properly, serves as the new family formed in Christ, and the elderly saints like Simeon and Anna in Luke's gospel are not alone.[4]

But somewhere in the middle of life, we fall prey to the illusion of our own self-sufficiency. Somewhere in the middle of life, the parents who used to take their kids to church no longer have kids living at home who need to be taken to church. What do many of them do when this moment arrives? More and more are staying home, going out to eat, or heading to the mountains to hike or ski. Church becomes just another one of many options, or worse, the thing that all those less fortunate people do who don't have the strength or financial resources to go it alone. The relational ties begin to loosen. Sure, they have some old friends with whom they raised their kids in the church, but there's no longer the active and dynamic interactions. We might arrogantly say things like, "I love Jesus but not the church," which is nonsense if indeed the church is his bride. To ignore the bride is to insult the groom.

One of the things that saddens me—frankly, bewilders me—is watching people live foolishly in peacetime, because those times won't last. At some point along the way, life will sneak up on all of us, and when it does, we will need the family of God to hold us up. But too many of us choose to live fragmented lives during the good years, separated from the life of the community, and then reach out for help only when the bottom falls out. If people want to live that way, that's their prerogative, and, of course, and the church ought to do whatever it can to help in such a moment. But can we just acknowledge that it's not ideal, and that it makes things harder? We forget how difficult it is to make new friends in crisis.

So let's go back for a moment and ask, What is the church, anyway? And why does it matter?

## Saint Jerome on Church

In the centuries following the ascension of the Lord Jesus, the mothers and fathers of the faith spent a lot of time wrestling with how to speak about the church. In the patristic period (roughly AD 100–750), the church fathers went to work by scouring through the Old Testament for clues. Since Paul himself insisted that "whatever was written [in the Old Testament] was written for our instruction" (Rom. 15:4 ESV), the church fathers borrowed those old Hebrew stories and turned their imaginations loose. They first read those stories *literally*, but then—and this is where things got really fun—they read them *allegorically*.

Saint Jerome (347–420), musing on the nature of the church, took up the story of Noah's ark. Like so many other biblical interpreters, Jerome saw Noah's ark as a "prefiguration" of the church; that is, the ark was a glimpse, a microcosm, and an anticipation of the church. In this ancient story, we find the story of the church in miniature. Just as every kind of animal was housed in the ark, so the church is made up of "every nation, tribe, people and language" (Rev. 7:9). In the ark were animals considered clean and unclean, just as in the church Jews and Gentiles are made one. And, like in the ark, in the church there is—or, at least, there ought to be—safety. What would normally be considered unsafe *outside* the ark, somehow held no threat of death *inside* the ark: "The wolf will live with the lamb, the leopard will lie down with the goat, the calf and the lion and the yearling together; and a little child will lead them" (Isa. 11:6). Jerome had to stop himself, stating finally, "The daylight would fail me if I were to explain all the mysteries of the ark and compare them with the Church."[5] The church, in short, is the container within which salvation is worked out.

More recently, Frederick Buechner picked up that same ancient allegory and developed it. In his book *Whistling in the Dark*, he points out that the architecture of medieval churches carried forward the story of Noah's ark. According to Buechner, the nave is the main section of the church where the congregation worships.[6] The word *nave* comes from the Latin word *navis*, which simply means "ship." It is the same word from which we derive *navy*.

The way the roof vaults in these old churches reminds one of an upside-down boat.[7]

For hundreds of years, the Catholic Church has been saying *"extra ecclesiam nulla salus,"* which means "outside the church there is no salvation." We Americans tend to think of the life of faith as the struggle of the rugged individual, but in the Bible, there are no rugged individuals who scratched and clawed their way into salvation. The story of the ark rules out the myth of individualism that we so cherish. Presumably, God could have doled out a bunch of canoes to a bunch of individuals to see who could fight their way through the storm. But instead, he gave us one boat, one church, one container of salvation that was open to all.

God graciously provides the boat, but he does not force anyone to get into it. And yet the invitation to come aboard is open to all.

## Jesus and the Church

I am bothered by the way we portray Jesus as some sort of individualistic freedom fighter who was disconnected from the worshiping life of Israel. The Gospels tell us a very different story. Jesus was out and about, mixing it up with sinners and saints. How much socializing did it take for Jesus to be accused of being a "glutton and a drunkard" (Matt. 11:19)? According to New Testament scholar Robert Karris, "In Luke's Gospel Jesus is either going to a meal, at a meal, or coming from a meal."[8]

And the Gospels explicitly tell us that Jesus consistently gathered with God's people:

> So [Jesus] came to Nazareth, where He had been brought up. And *as His custom was*, He went into the synagogue on the Sabbath day, and stood up to read. (Luke 4:16 NKJV, emphasis mine)

Instead of "as His custom was," we might say today that he was "a regular churchgoer." And this detail from Luke was not an isolated event either. Jesus was in the temple often, counting the offerings (Luke 21:1–4) and teaching them as one who had great authority (Mark 6:2; Luke 13:10). As the psalmist said about the Messiah who would come, "Zeal for your house consumes me" (Ps. 69:9). King David himself said, "As for the saints in the land, they are the excellent ones, in whom is all my delight" (Ps. 16:3 ESV). Jesus is the one who confronted Saul and turned him into Paul, who would later write, "as we have opportunity, let us do good to all people, *especially to those who belong to the family of believers*" (Gal. 6:10, emphasis mine).

Jesus was a man of the church, and if church was good enough for Jesus, it ought to be good enough for us.

## The One Thing We Have Going for Us

Let me say this: I know why so many people have difficulty with the thought of going to church. For the last
two millennia, too many church leaders have given people
plenty of reasons to mistrust the church. Some people
have come to church longing to find the glorious Father,
only to hear sermons about a vicious and angry God who
is looking for ways to destroy our lives. Some people have
come to church looking for shelter from the madness of
their own broken families, only to suffer abuse at the
hands of a priest or pastor. Some people have come to
church looking to share their resources so that the family
of God can be a blessing to the world, only to find shady
shepherds mishandling the funds. So I understand why
some people have difficulty trusting the church. I myself
have experienced great pain within the family of God,
and I would never say anything to minimize others' experiences. I grieve with those who have suffered, and the
Father in heaven grieves the wound inflicted on us.

Some people, having experienced such pain, will want
to do away with the church altogether and will say things
like, "Come on, you and I both know that the church is
full of hypocrites! They're no better than the world outside of the church." Yes, they are exactly right. The church
has its share of hypocrites and sinners. But Jesus himself

showed us that he came to unite hypocrites and sinners. There they all are, in the Upper Room with Jesus on the night he was betrayed: Peter, who talked out of both sides of his mouth. At dinner he confidently shouted, "I'll never deny you, Lord!" only to deny even knowing Jesus three times a few hours later. Judas, who sat there at the table eating the bread and drinking the wine while his pockets were lined with blood money. Jesus surely knew all of it. He could have cleared out the room. But for some reason, he allowed these guys to come close and fed them. For God so loved the world that he decided to make space for people like Peter and Judas, for people like you and me.

Yes, we are no better than the world outside the church, but we do have one thing going for us: we believe in Jesus. We believe that Jesus, through his death and resurrection, has conquered the power of sin and death, and he will raise us up with him at the last day. We believe that Jesus became fully human and, in his obedience to the Father, has made obedience possible for all of us. We believe that the church has faithfully passed on God's Word to us, and so we let him transform us. We believe that Jesus has given us his Spirit to guide us all along the way.

In short, we believe that Jesus knows what to do with haggard old sinners like us, so *as the church*, we gather together weekly *in the church*, and let him make something of us.

## So Why Go to Church?

The brilliant Australian theologian Dr. Ben Myers was asked many years ago why he goes to church. He summed it up well:

> I do not go to church because it is enjoyable (usually it's not), or because it is never dull (usually it is). I do not go to church because it satisfies my private needs and wishes (it seldom does). I do not go to church for myself. I go because of Adam.[9]

What does it mean for us to go to church "because of Adam"? Adam and Eve, the first family in the garden of Eden, were deceived by the tempter and lured away into a kind of life that devolves into nonbeing. For that is what sin does. It unmakes us, destroys us, and sinks us—and the creation around us—back into chaos. Many people today are uncomfortable with the concept of sin, and like to think that they have "progressed" past those primitive concepts into a state of "greater enlightenment."[10] They can ignore the reality all they want, but the First Adam is still very much in our bones, and he must be repeatedly cast out.

In some places, churchgoing folks experience the scorn—or at least the sideways glances—of coworkers, neighbors, and others who think going to church is a sign of weakness or simplemindedness. Saint Peter wasn't being hyperbolic when he wrote to the believers scattered around the Mediterranean basin: "But ye are a chosen generation, a royal priesthood, an holy nation, *a peculiar people*" (1 Peter 2:9 KJV, emphasis mine). He wanted to prepare them. He was letting them know that their affiliation with Jesus and his church would make them look strange to the nations around them. And strange the church has looked, for Karl Marx once famously called religion "the opiate of the masses."[11] Others have called the church a "crutch" for the feeble, for those who don't have enough strength on their own to carry them through. Dr. Ben Myers addresses this accusation unflinchingly:

> Yes, religion is a crutch. But it's not my own personal crutch. It is Adam's crutch. It's the human race that walks (if it walks at all) with a limp. And so when Sunday morning comes around I drag old Adam out of bed. I make him get dressed and put shoes on his feet. I brush his teeth. I lead him out the door. I force him to go to church. It's a thankless task, but somebody's got to do it. I expect that if I keep dragging Adam along to church every Sunday, he might eventually become a Christian. And if he becomes a Christian— who knows?—perhaps in time he will even become

that rarest and best of things: a genuine, proper, fully functioning and bona fide human being.[12]

If you follow Jesus, then get yourself up on Sunday mornings, wash your face, and go to church. Put yourself in the way of the saints who have what you need. Realize that in staying away from the church, *you* are missing out. And go to church so you can put yourself in the way of those who need what you have. Realize also that when you stay away from the church, *others* are missing out. Every week, come ready to give and to receive.

Don't be foolish in peacetime. Be wise. Gather with the saints. Fall in love with the church. When you go to church, make it your goal to change someone's day. Pray for one person. Have a beautiful conversation with one person. Be kind to a rambunctious child. Help an elderly person to the car. Buy someone a coffee and give them an encouraging word. I'm not asking you to make some sort of Herculean effort. I'm inviting you to live out your vocation as a part of the body of Christ. It's the only way we can grow as Christians. It's the only way to develop the friends we will need in the foxhole.

# SIX

# The Wisdom of
# a Quiet Life

Love to be unknown.

—Thomas à Kempis (1380–1471)

Make it your ambition to lead a quiet life.

—Saint Paul (1 Thess. 4:11)

**W**itnessing the proliferation of mass media, Andy
Warhol, the enigmatic mid-twentieth-century pop
artist, said, "In the future, everyone will be world-famous

for fifteen minutes." That was 1968. Warhol had no idea just how right he would be.

For most of human history, the majority of people were confined to one geographical space. They had no other option than to be okay with blending in, with playing their part in the intricate tapestry of human relationships. Local villagers were required to know the rural farmers on the outskirts of town. They would barter, engage in the mutual exchange of goods and services, and participate in the back-and-forth of life. Yes, there were politicians and generals and power brokers, but most people lived a simple, quiet life of working for their daily bread.

To our modern ears, that kind of life can sound like a punishment. But down through the ages, great poets and philosophers, luminous saints and legendary sages, all have held the quiet life in high esteem. Far from being something all those "less fortunate" people get stuck with, the quiet life is something every wise person pursues.

In fact, many people who get swept up into a life of public notoriety often come to regret, even detest, it later. Think of the countless children who became television stars before cratering beneath the pressure. Think of Michael Oher, the NFL offensive lineman who rose to fame after the hit movie *The Blind Side* released in theaters. He was being flown around to press junkets, the movie grossed over $300 million, and Sandra Bullock

won an Oscar and a Golden Globe award for her performance. However, in an interview only a few years later,
Oher said he was "tired of the movie."

> Offensive linemen don't get looked at. Nobody is pay-
> ing attention to the offensive line. But me? I'm getting
> watched for everything. . . . That's taken away from my
> football. That's why people criticize me. That's why
> people look at me every single play. . . . This stuff,
> calling me a bust, people saying if I can play or not . . .
> that has nothing to do with football. It's something else
> off the field. That's why I don't like that movie.[1]

Fame favors the few and destroys many. In a satirical
reversal of Andy Warhol's prediction, British street artist
Banksy wrote in graffiti: "In the future, everyone will be
anonymous for 15 minutes."[2]

## The Wisdom of Albert Einstein

It was 1922, and Albert Einstein was traveling the world
on a speaking tour. The German-born physicist was in
the running to win the Nobel Peace Prize for his ground-
breaking work in explaining the photoelectric effect,
which is the science behind what we now know as solar

energy. He was in Tokyo, Japan, and the place was packed with adoring crowds. The excitement was palpable. After the people departed, he made his way back to the Imperial Hotel. A mail carrier was waiting for him in the lobby with a message that it was official: Einstein had won the Nobel Peace Prize!

Upon receiving the letter, he reached into his pocket for a tip but realized he didn't have any money. Embarrassed, and wanting to give the messenger something, he grabbed some hotel stationery and a pen and wrote out two phrases. He told the carrier that he hoped the two little pieces of paper would be worth something someday. What did he write?

The first note said: "Where there's a will, there's a way."

The second note said: "A calm and humble life will bring more happiness than the pursuit of success and the constant restlessness that comes with it."

This is the wisdom of a man who spent his life tucked away in laboratories, but who was now trying to figure out what to do with the newfound fame and recognition. I wonder if his second piece of advice—a return to "a calm and humble life"—was what he was hoping for. In 2017, the two notes from Einstein were sold at an auction by a family member of the deceased courier for $1.8 million! While that's certainly a lot of money, the wisdom given in the note is priceless.[3]

## The Most Popular Book by the
## Most Unknown Saint

In 1380, in the small Rhineland town of Kempen, Germany, a young boy named Thomas was born into the Hammercken family. We know very little about his family, but we know that Thomas attended a religious school across the border in Deventer, Holland. He excelled in his studies, and, as with the four young Hebrew boys in Nebuchadnezzar's Babylon, God gave him "knowledge and understanding of all kinds of literature and learning" (Dan. 1:17). Thomas was deeply committed to a life of prayer, and when he turned nineteen, he took vows and moved into the monastery at Mount Saint Agnes in Zwolle, Holland.

Along with his daily chores of cooking, cleaning, and maintaining the monastery's garden, Thomas was assigned to teach the novices—the prospective priests who were hoping to be accepted into the priesthood, but who were in a period of discerning whether or not they had been called to make the lifelong vow—about their proper work and the correct posturing of their attitudes toward the monastic life. In order to do this, he wrote them letters. This was by no means glamorous work, but it needed doing, and Thomas did it with utmost seriousness. In the early 1400s, he wrote four booklets to these young priests. In one of them he said,

As long as you live, you will be subject to change, whether you will it or not—now glad, now sorrowful; now pleased, now displeased; now devout, now undevout; now vigorous, now slothful; now gloomy, now merry. But a wise man who is well taught in spiritual labor stands unshaken in all such things, and heeds little what he feels, or from what side the wind of instability blows.[4]

Thomas wanted to deromanticize the life of the monastery. He knew that the priesthood was fraught with ups and downs, so he warned them and called them to steady faithfulness. Thomas was a good writer, and his letters brim over with memorable axioms:

A humble rustic who serves God is better than a proud intellectual who neglects his soul to study the course of the stars.[5]

It is no very small matter, therefore, for a man to forsake himself even in things that are very small.[6]

All men desire peace, but all do not care for the things that go to make true peace.[7]

But perhaps one of my favorite lines from Thomas is this simple phrase that has haunted me since the day I first read it two decades ago:

Love to be unknown and considered as nothing.[8]

In all his searching and reaching out to God in prayer, and in all his study of the way of Jesus, Thomas came up with something so simple and yet so profound: "Love to be unknown." In our self-promoting society, I wonder if we have forgotten how to trust Jesus to be the superintendent of our stories. We have forgotten that saints have always been willing to be the best-kept secrets, stealthily sneaking around and giving life to the world. Thomas takes it even a step further:

> Anyone, then, who aims to live the inner and spiritual life must go apart, with Jesus, from the crowd. No man appears in safety before the public eye unless he first relishes obscurity. No man is safe in speaking unless he loves to be silent. No man rules safely unless he is willing to be ruled. No man commands safely unless he has learned well how to obey. No man rejoices safely unless he has within him the testimony of a good conscience.[9]

Yes, we are talking about Thomas all these years later. But don't forget that he was a man who lived what he taught, who was almost entirely unknown to those outside the four walls of the monastery, save a few close friends and family members. He wasn't "on the radar," and he didn't have great influence during his lifetime. After his death in July 1471, his letters were collected, bound together in book form, and called *The Imitation of Christ*, which was the title of his first letter to the novices. For some reason—and all it takes is reading a few pages to see why—the book started circulating. It was translated and sent to monasteries all over the region. It grew wings and flew to the four corners of the earth. Ignatius of Loyola, founder of the Jesuit movement, was said to have read a chapter every day. John Wesley thought it contained the clearest description of the life of faith and was known to give copies away.[10] In fact, *The Imitation of Christ* is the second most-translated and second highest-selling book in the history of Christendom—second only to the Bible. Thomas himself never saw financial gain from his letters, which is fitting for the life he called us to live.

We now know him as Saint Thomas à Kempis, but his fellow priests knew him simply as Thomas. There is a great irony here of the kingdom-of-God sort: the most popular book was written by one of the most obscure saints.

## Finding Jesus in the Fields of Obscurity

Have you ever taken a moment to consider just how odd it is that we know almost nothing about the first thirty years of Jesus' life? We have exactly *two stories* recorded in the four Gospels that give us only a sparse glimpse of Jesus before his public ministry was launched.

The first time we hear about Jesus is when he was circumcised in the temple when he was eight days old (Luke 2:21–24). Because every Jewish boy was circumcised on the eighth day, this seems like a detail that's hardly worth noting. This revelation doesn't elevate Jesus above everyone else to a place of transcendent power; rather, it situates him immanently *within* the people of God by showing that his life had been *given over to* the Mosaic tradition. It sounds like it was a good day at church for the eight-day-old Jesus and his family as the old sage, Simeon, took up the child in his arms and sang the song of salvation, and the elderly prophetess Anna "gave thanks to God and spoke about the child to all who were looking forward to the redemption of Jerusalem" (Luke 2:38). But that's it! That's the first gospel story written about the little boy Jesus. His parents took him to church, and he got circumcised.

The second time we hear about Jesus is when Mary and Joseph had to file a missing child report for him when he was twelve years old. As the story goes, they had made their yearly pilgrimage to Jerusalem for the Feast of the Passover. But when the feast was over and their group of relatives and friends started their slow journey back home to Galilee, for a full day, Mary and Joseph failed to discover that Jesus was not among them. There was a lot happening, as in any traveling company, so it's understandable that they thought Jesus was in their company before realizing he had actually stayed behind in Jerusalem (Luke 2:43–44). Mary and Joseph had lost track of the Son of God! This is one of those stories to be filed under the "you had one job" folder. But Jesus was just fine, and when they found him three days later, he was "in the temple courts, sitting among the teachers, listening to them and asking them questions" (Luke 2:46).

These two stories of the young Jesus have so much to teach us, the least of which is this: God can be up to something beautiful with your life even if the world knows almost nothing about you. Think about Joseph being sold into slavery by his very own flesh and blood and imprisoned in a foreign land before being put in charge of all of Egypt. Think about Moses living on the backside of the Midian wilderness for forty years before being called to lead his people out of Egypt. Think about the young shepherd boy David, who was hidden away in the fields of obscurity before becoming king of Israel. Think about Jesus' own mother, Mary, who was surely one of the invisible figures of her day until the archangel Gabriel showed up.

## Developing Holy Indifference

Saint Paul of Tarsus had internalized the reality by the time he wrote to the Thessalonian believers living on the coast of Greece:

> Now about your love for one another we do not need to write to you, for you yourselves have been taught by God to love each other. And in fact, you do love all of God's family throughout Macedonia. Yet we urge you, brothers and sisters, to do so more and more, and *to make it your ambition to lead a quiet life*: You should mind your own business and work with your hands, just as we told you, so that your daily life may win the respect of outsiders and so that you will not be dependent on anybody. (1 Thess. 4:9–12, emphasis mine)

Paul wrote another letter, this time to his young apprentice Timothy, encouraging him to carve out regular time in his prayer closet. He instructed Timothy to pray and intercede "for kings and all those in authority, *that we may live peaceful and quiet lives* in all godliness and holiness. This is good, and pleases God our Savior" (1 Tim. 2:2–3, emphasis mine). But Paul's words, at first, seem contradictory to us. Being ambitious about living quietly is a puzzle that not many of us are ready to solve. We are living in a land of loud self-promotion. The way of this world goes something like this: Get out there. Change the world. Do it big. Make a splash. Get a reality TV show if you can. But the way of God's kingdom runs in the opposite direction: Lay your life down. Care for your neighbor. Honor the elderly. Visit the forgotten. Give your money away. Deflect praise. Wash the feet of the world. These are the precepts of two kingdoms, diverging in radically opposite directions. While the art of living quietly seems to be passing away right in front of our eyes, the saints are those who have been trained in the art of not caring one bit, who have learned to develop a holy indifference to it all.

We find Jesus regularly sending away the crowds. I can imagine the disciples' bewilderment. *Jesus, don't you know we could have capitalized on the energy of that moment! We've got a brand to build, a movement to galvanize.* We find Jesus refusing to cozy up to the political leaders of his day. One gets the feeling that he wasn't jockeying for front-page write-ups in the leading media outlets. Instead, we read about him intrepidly escaping into the hills to find the acclaim of the only One who mattered: his Father (Matt. 14:23; Luke 5:16, 6:12, 9:28–29).

## On Telling Bono to Wait

Eugene Peterson is one of the last of a generation of saints who had the courage to go slowly, who had the faith to live in obscurity. We have forgotten that it takes great faith to live small. Eugene spent twenty-nine years tending a flock of saints in Bel Air, Maryland, before the world knew about him. It wasn't until the publication of *The Message* that he became known. I've been saying for years that it only took Eugene Peterson sixty-five years to become an "overnight success."

Yet, even after he became well-known, he ran from the spotlight and turned down opportunities that most of us would chase. This is the man who said no to an invitation from Bono, the world's most iconic rock star, because he was too busy translating Isaiah.[11] Sure, in the last few years of his life they got together and formed a beautiful friendship—but not until it was *time*. Eugene was never in a hurry.

But I'm afraid that much of pastoral ministry, as it is practiced in America today, is marked by our impatience with the kingdom's pace of life. Instead of giving ourselves over to anonymity, we admire—and some even strive for—celebrity. While Jesus stripped himself of his robe to wash the feet of the world, many of our leaders in the church are recognized as fashion icons. Eugene called us to live the *Jesus way*, but every day, we're seeing how easy it is to tell the story of the humiliated Jesus with all the hubris of Caesar Augustus.

Father Ronald Rolheiser, the Catholic priest and quiet sage, diagnoses our age as one of "narcissism . . . and unbridled restlessness."[12]

> In this posture of unbridled restlessness, we stand before life too greedy, too full of expectations that cannot be realized, and unable to accept that, here, in this life, all symphonies remain unfinished. We are unable to rest or be satisfied because we are convinced that all lack, all tension, and all unfulfilled yearning is tragic.[13]

Our society trains us to *want it all* and to *want it now*. But Rolheiser says, "When we are obsessed in this way it is hard to be contemplative."[14] Because Eugene Peterson had spent his life chasing the wisdom of the saints, he knew that they regularly commended us to a life of restraint, a life of fasting not only from food but from opportunities to be known, and of forgoing opportunities to gain power at the wrong time and in the wrong way. Eugene didn't build his own brand; he waited on the Lord. He lived a quiet life. And the quiet life is good because it puts us squarely behind Jesus as he walks up into the hills to pray.

The quiet life is good because it trains us to trust in the timing and provision of God and not in our own ability to "make things happen" for ourselves. The quiet life is good because it is only when we get quiet that we begin to hear the "still small voice [of God]" (1 Kings 19:12 NKJV).

One of Israel's great psalmists teaches us a prayer that can carry us through when we get restless and feel overlooked and forgotten. It is a prayer that nurtures quiet contentment and serves as an antidote to the agitation we feel when we are faced with our own hiddenness. It is a prayer that lets God know that we trust him with the trajectory of our lives, no matter how simple. And here's the prayer:

The boundary lines have fallen for me in pleasant places; surely I have a delightful inheritance. (Ps. 16:6)

Take those words onto your lips, let them sink into your heart, and learn the wisdom of living a quiet life.

# SEVEN

# The Wisdom of an Old Library

*This is what the* LORD *says:*

*"Stand at the crossroads and look;*
  *ask for the ancient paths,*
*ask where the good way is, and walk in it,*
  *and you will find rest for your souls."*

—Jeremiah 6:16

**W**hen I showed up at Eugene Peterson's house for my first visit, he met me at the front door and welcomed me in. We exchanged pleasantries, doing what everyone does as they work to get a feel for each other. After a few minutes he showed me to my room to get settled. I unpacked my bag in disbelief that I was actually staying with the Petersons for the next three days. Then we went into his study, a modest but stunning rectangular room with windows overlooking Montana's Flathead Lake. It was a sanctuary for the gods of literature. Books lined the left wall as you walked in, a floor-to-ceiling catalogue of the Christian tradition.

I asked if I could thumb through some of the books. "Of course," he said, as he sat down in his rocking chair. There was Karl Barth's entire collection of *Church Dogmatics*, which Eugene told me he had read through three times. There was a J. R. R. Tolkien section and a C. S. Lewis section. Hans Urs von Balthasar, Wendell Berry, and Gerard Manley Hopkins lined the walls. He was in possession of everything Saints Teresa of Avila and Hildegard of Bingen had ever written. I turned to the dog-eared pages and read the handwritten notes in the margins. These books evidently had been digested through multiple readings. Eugene sat quietly in the corner of the study, gliding back and forth in his rocking chair. Then out of the silence came his voice: "Read the dead people," he said.

Petroleum geologists are paid good money to poke and prod our planet in hopes of discovering reserves of organic-rich shale that have been cooked by the earth's core and turned into hydrocarbons, the ever-coveted oil and natural gas. Whoever strikes oil first, wins. It's big money. Some even call it "black gold." But Eugene had discovered that the most valuable—and maybe the most overlooked—natural resources are usually found only six feet under the ground, in the graves of those who have gone before us, and in the books they have left us. "Read the dead people."

Many of the ancient books that have become treasures to the church must be excavated, as they are often buried underneath the rubble of a thousand pop bestsellers with which our bookshelves runneth over. Borrowing the words of Jesus, many of the books we read *first* because of their slick marketing allure should be read *last*, and some of the books placed *last* on our list should be *first*. Eugene told me to "read the dead people" because their work has been "tested by more than one generation and been given passing marks. That means that what these Christians have written has been validated by something deeper than fashion or fad."[1]

## Finding the Old Trails

I have spent the last fourteen years living in the Rocky Mountains of Southern Colorado. The Rockies find their point of origin where I live and stretch all the way up through Wyoming, Montana, and into the rugged landscapes of Canada. Colorado alone has fifty-four mountain peaks that rise above 14,000 feet in elevation, and every weekend people head for the hills to see if they can reach the summit. I wake up every morning looking at the "purple mountain majesties" of Pikes Peak, which never gets old.

These mountains can take your breath away, but they can also take your life away. Mountains are beautiful *and* austere, a gratuitous gift from God *and* a dangerous pursuit of mankind. Because of the danger, expert guides have gone ahead and worked diligently to delineate safe trails for hobby hikers like me. They have posted warning signs and repaired shoddy trails. They have created GPS coordinates that can be followed, mapping the way so those who come after them can experience the joy of the journey safely.

There is a beautiful austerity about the life of faith as well. There are moments that will take your breath away, but there are also slippery slopes that will destroy you if you're not careful. Mercifully, we are not the first people to walk the trail. Somewhere around 627 BC, Jeremiah of Anathoth was unexpectedly unsettled by the Spirit of the Lord. It must have been just another day until the Lord came crashing in on him and thrust him out onto the prophetic path.

"Before I formed you in the womb I knew you,
    before you were born I set you apart;
    I appointed you as a prophet to the nations."

                                                (Jer. 1:5)

By the time God came looking for Jeremiah, the people of Israel were in a bad way. They had lost their true north. The darkness they were stumbling through was a self-inflicted wound that had been brought about by their waywardness. The people who had been chosen to carry God's blessing to the world had been carried off into exile. And into the void came Yahweh's voice:

This is what the LORD says:

"Stand at the crossroads and look;
    *ask for the ancient paths,*
    *ask where the good way is,* and walk in it,
    and you will find rest for your souls."

                                    (Jer. 6:16, emphasis mine)

As we scan our literary history, a constellation of metaphors clusters together that demonstrates how we speak of finding entrance into the good life. The good life is lived into as we embark on the long and arduous journey down *the road* (or path, trail, way). We think of life as a prolonged pilgrimage, and the enduring popularity of John Bunyan's *The Pilgrim's Progress* shows just how much we long to find our way.

In the book of Job, we read:

> Ask the former generation
> and find out what their ancestors learned,
> for we were born only yesterday and know nothing,
> and our days on earth are but a shadow.
> Will they not instruct you and tell you?
> Will they not bring forth words from their
> understanding?
>
> (Job 8:8–10)

There are ancient paths that ought to be found. There is a "good way" that all are invited to walk. There is a life of elemental wholesomeness and vitality, a kind of life that can rise above the besetting sins and cheap seductions that have thrown many lives off course. There is a life that can weather every storm. And isn't that what all of us are longing for?

In my experience, it's the older saints who have discovered the way, who have heeded the call to walk the ancient paths. They went before us, have climbed the mountain of God, have walked the often treacherous path of holiness, jamming signposts into solid earth and leaving clues along the trail. They have written down their parables and allegories and timeless stories. Think of Dante's *Divine Comedy* (1321). Think of Milton's *Paradise Lost* (1667), Dickens's *A Tale of Two Cities* (1859), and even Lewis's *The Lion, the Witch, and the Wardrobe* (1950).

These books call to us: *Watch out. Pay attention. Caution ahead. Keep your eyes open.* They have preserved for us the clues, the wisdom they gathered along the way. Wise are the ones who avail themselves of those resources.

## The Threat in Our Own Time

Reading is one of the great delights of human existence. When things are working right, we open our hearts as we open a book and set out on a journey of discovery, which can sometimes even lead to transformation. But reading, as the saints prescribe, is being threatened in our time. The problem is not that people have *stopped* reading, but that our cultural moment threatens to significantly impoverish our reading. Because of the information age in which we live, our reading habits have changed dramatically. People are reading plenty of *words*—an amalgamation of social media posts, sports updates, celebrity gossip, and senseless trivia—but fewer *books*.[2]

Words have been taken hostage and pressed into the

service of "breaking news" marketers. Words breathlessly race across the bottom of our screens with the news of category-five hurricanes or with the announcement that the Dow Jones was up five points. Text messages and push notifications magically throw words up onto our phones, and our coworkers feel the tremors as the boardroom table is in a constant state of vibration. We are a society being buzzed, zapped, and alerted to death. Words litter the landscape of our lives like chaff on a threshing floor.

Pragmatists and utilitarians have trained us to believe that words primarily need to be *useful*, but ask yourself, When was the last time you found words to be *beautiful*? We all know that words are constantly filling up our inboxes, but when was the last time words filled your *hearts* or took over your imagination? We all know that words race to the four corners of the globe at the speed of one's fiber-optic connection, but when was the last time words stopped you in your tracks? In our moment in time, it is possible to do a lot of reading without ever really reading much.

I am not trying to be nostalgic or to romanticize the past. We are living in a digital age, and I am quite aware that there is no going back. But I do believe words can be hallowed again in our time, and I believe a necessary resistance must be staged against the insurgent forces seeking to cheapen our engagement with words. There are at least two forces at play that are worth considering: our close friendship with distraction, and our love of novelty.

## Our Friendship with Distraction

We are a people easily distracted. The technologically advanced Western world—I'll speak for myself and from my own context—is a world of overstimulation, and at times, a full-on assault to the senses. It is no secret that there is an overwhelming amount of information available these days. Unlike previous generations that had to go to a public or university library to acquire information, we carry the information around in our pockets, have it right at our fingertips. Research suggests that the technological advances we've experienced are not without negative effects; they are not neutral. In 2017, the scientific journal *Frontiers in Psychology* published a study entitled "Smartphones and Cognition," in which researchers showed that *"even the mere awareness of* the physical presence of a cell phone may impact cognitive performance"[3] (emphasis mine). They discovered that a cell phone doesn't even have to ring or buzz for our cognitive performance to be diminished. The phone just has to *be there*. We wonder if a new email has come in. We wonder what we might be missing out on in the world of geopolitics, sports, and even friendships. The study goes on:

Perhaps the most recognizable, and obvious, impact of smartphone technology in our everyday lives is the way in which it can acutely interfere with, or interrupt, ongoing mental and physical tasks. . . . Once attention has been shifted to the smartphone for one purpose, *users often then engage in a chain of subsequent task-unrelated acts on the smartphone, thereby extending the period of disruption.* Studies exploring these "within-phone" interruptions have found that task completion in one app can be delayed by up to 400% by an unintended interruption from another app. . . . The researchers posited that the notifications prompted task-irrelevant thoughts, which manifested themselves in poorer performance on the primary task.[4]

"Task-unrelated acts" and "task-irrelevant thoughts" are the new realities of our lives and our workforce. Another study suggests that these "drifts of attention might arise from a desire for more immediate gratification" when the monotony of the workday wears on.[5] Discovering someone liked our post on Twitter or our picture on Facebook gives us the dopamine hit that feels so good. It takes us into another imaginative world, but not without first evacuating us from another domain, such as work, family, relationships, and so on.

This allure affects us all. In her witty article "Internet

Distraction: The Writer's Main Dilemma," veteran novelist Kristen Houghton observes, "Being a good writer is 3% hard work and 97% not getting distracted by the Internet."[6] Clearly there's a bit of hyperbole in her statement, but as one who has written a book, I can tell you that she may not be that far off. The great seventeenth-century mathematician and theologian Blaise Pascal summed it up well when he said, "All of humanity's problems stem from man's inability to sit quietly in a room alone."[7]

### Our Love of Novelty

Written in 1596, Shakespeare's *Merchant of Venice* remains a timeless story. Portia, the young protagonist of the story, is a woman of great wealth, noble birth, and considerable beauty. Her father has died, and in his will, he set forth the terms of how she is to find her husband. Three caskets would be placed in front of her suitors, but only one would have her picture in it. Whoever picked that one would win the right to have her hand in marriage. One casket was made of gold, one of silver, and the other of unattractive lead. Each casket had an inscription on top of it. The first two seemed promising, while the last one wasn't very appealing:

Gold: "Who chooseth me shall gain what many men desire."

Silver: "Who chooseth me shall get as much as he deserves."

Lead: "Who chooseth me must give and hazard all he hath."[8]

Noblemen from the four winds of the earth came calling, hoping to win Portia's heart, and some, seeking her money. One potential suitor was the Prince of Morocco, a flamboyant and conceited character who believed he *deserved* Portia. "I do in birth deserve her, and in fortunes, in graces and in qualities of breeding."[9] Because he thought of himself as the gold standard, he naturally chose the golden casket. But in it he found a skull, a sign of death, and a scroll that opened with these words: "All that glitters is not gold. . . . Gilded tombs do worms enfold." We could stand to learn this lesson afresh today. Shakespeare presumably had a young audience in mind, for both Portia and the Prince were "young in limbs." And though they be "young in limbs," they can be "in judgment old." In the end, the youthful Prince of Morocco chose wrongly and was therefore disqualified.

Like the Prince of Morocco, we, too, tend to be drawn to all that shimmers. We love everything that glitters with the radiance of novelty. We hear about a new gadget, a new line of clothing, or a new skin-care product and have it drop-shipped to our front doors in forty-eight hours. We discover new celebrities cropping up every month, and because they have a few hundred thousand followers on social media, we allow ourselves to be tricked into thinking they automatically have something to say. Young musicians and artists become our spokespeople for what the "good life" looks like, and they usually tell us it involves riches, travel, good food, and slim bodies.

Even in the church, we lionize our young preachers who aren't even old enough to have a kid in high school. Novelty, novelty, novelty. All the while we ignore so many of our sages and older saints who actually *do* have something to say; we ignore the ancient paths. Before Shakespeare, King Solomon told us that there is "nothing new under the sun" (Eccl. 1:9). And Jesus repeatedly taught us to develop a healthy mistrust of all that glitters that isn't really gold.

## The Great Cloud of Literary Witnesses

The writer of Hebrews introduced us to the "great cloud of witnesses" who have gone before us (chaps. 11–12). We read about Abel and Enoch, Noah and Abraham; we're provoked by the lives of Sarah and Rahab; we remember Jacob, who became Israel, and Moses, the deliverer. We cannot forget where we came from. Yes, in a strange way, looking back helps us as we move forward. And I like to think of "reading the dead people" as an act of getting caught up in the great cloud of *literary* witnesses.

There are certain saints whose lives must be remembered. There are certain stories that need to be read. While I would never pretend to be able to construct a definitive list of "required reading" for Christians, for the sake of those who would like some help, please allow me to make some suggestions. Any of these will be a good place to start. And as you read them, they will introduce you to other "dead saints" whom you might want to chase down:

- Walk the trails of Tunisia in the year AD 203 and get to know Perpetua and Felicitas, two women who were some of the early Christian martyrs. Their faithfulness and heroism in the face of crushing adversity ought to wake any of us up. There are many books detailing their story, including *The Acts of the Christian Martyrs*, trans. Herbert Musurillo (New York: Oxford University Press, 1972). For a brief summary, go to https://www.pbs.org/wgbh/pages/frontline /shows/religion/maps/primary/perpetua.html.

- Journey back to fourth-century Algeria and read Saint Augustine's *Confessions*, wherein he catalogues his early years of egregious rebellion that were no match for the God whose love is relentless. Saint

Augustine, *Confessions*, trans. Henry Chadwick (New York: Oxford University Press, 2009).

- Read about Saint Macrina, a Turkish woman from the fourth century who helped raise two of the church's great theologians: Saint Basil the Great and Saint Gregory of Nyssa. She was their older sister, and when Gregory was asked who shaped his life, his first response was Macrina. He thought so highly of her that he wrote, "A life of this quality should not be forgotten for the future." Gregory of Nyssa, *The Life of Saint Macrina* (Eugene, OR: Wipf & Stock, 2001), 21.
- Consider what it might have cost Martin Luther in the 1500s to say, "Here I stand, I can do no other, so help me God" in the face of such great opposition. Luther, *The Bondage of the Will* (Ada, MI: Baker Academic, 2012).
- Take some time and get acquainted with Brother Lawrence, the seventeenth-century French Carmelite monk who taught us the art of "practicing the presence of God in one single act that does not end." Brother Lawrence, *The Practice of the Presence of God* (New Kensington, PA: Whitaker House, 1982).
- Learn how to pray with the Puritans. Arthur Bennett, ed., *The Valley of Vision: A Collection of Puritan Prayers and Devotions* (Edinburgh: The Banner of Truth Trust, 1975).

- Learn the cost of discipleship from Dietrich Bonhoeffer, a man who died a Christian martyr at the hands of Nazi Germany. Bonhoeffer, *The Cost of Discipleship* (New York: Touchstone, 1995).
- Read Dr. Martin Luther King Jr.'s sermons and get swept up into fighting for the oppressed. *A Gift of Love: Sermons from Strength to Love and Other Preachings*, King Legacy series (Boston: Beacon Press, 2012).

Some books you read for information; other books scrub you clean and stand you back up on your feet. The books I have mentioned can do just that.

## But Why Read the Ancients?

Why is reading the works of "dead" writers so helpful? What do they have that contemporary writers don't? What is the benefit? What does doing so do to us or train us to do? We submit ourselves to older writers because their counsel lives *outside* the conventional wisdom of our age. They speak to us, in essence, from a different world; they give us wisdom from a seasoned perspective. They have a hard-won wisdom to share with us that was born out of adversities our generation will never face.

Many of these ancient writers lived in dire poverty. Most of them never achieved renown in their own day but have only become known *after* their deaths, which ensures a purity of motive on the part of the writers. Many of these ancient writers were bi-vocational, working a job during the day to put food on the table while carving out time to write. Many lived in nations and cultures completely different from our own, so their experience and wisdom broaden our horizons and help us envision new possibilities, even as we live the lives God set us down in.

And think about what it took for their letters and papers to find their way to us. Think about the almost insurmountable odds of survival facing Saint Thomas's simple letters that became *The Imitation of Christ*. Think about what it must have taken for Saint Augustine's *Confessions* from the fourth century to survive the decay of a technologically impoverished world so that we could read them! But they *did* survive. That's because a whole bunch of people thought their letters were worth preserving. Our ancestors saw their words as necessary directives, important clues for the human journey, and made sure to pass them on to us. Wisdom says we should read them.

What does reading the ancient writers do to us and for us? Perhaps, most importantly, it trains us in humility by placing us in the position to be learners. It reminds us that we come from somewhere, that we're not making up this whole life-of-faith thing as we go. It reminds us that we are a part of the "one, holy, universal and apostolic" church that we all proclaim in the Nicene Creed.

Reading the ancient writers introduces us to the crises the church has faced throughout the centuries, and it shows us how they responded. Our crises won't be exactly the same as theirs, but as we pay attention to our history, as we spend more time in the practice room, we are "learning the scales" that will prepare us to improvise when our own crises come our way.

## The Bones of Joseph

In the Exodus narrative, we find Moses preparing to lead the people out of Egypt. After four hundred years of slavery, they couldn't get out of there fast enough. But before Moses left town, he made one final stop. This detail should not be missed:

> *Moses took the bones of Joseph with him,* for Joseph had made the Israelites solemnly swear to do it, saying, "God will surely hold you accountable, *so make sure you bring my bones from here with you.*" (Ex. 13:19 THE MESSAGE)

Many years before the exodus, Joseph, one of Israel's sons, was sold into slavery by his brothers, whose jealousy spilled over into unconscionable cruelty. The hits kept on coming for Joseph, and he soon found himself imprisoned in Egypt. Though his environment was entirely hostile, Joseph figured out how to maintain his faithful witness in an unfaithful land, and he eventually rose to become Pharaoh's second-in-command. Toward the end of his life, Joseph stated his final wish: "take my bones with you as you leave here" (Gen. 50:25 THE MESSAGE). So, before Moses charged out of Egypt and into the unknown, he took a detour to Joseph's grave. He exhumed his remains and carried them with him all the way into the promised land.

I think the practice of "reading the dead people" is a similar act. They may have entered their rest, but we can still carry them with us. We can preserve their legacies. We can remember, cherish, and pass on their wisdom to the people coming after us.

## Where to Go from Here

After reading this chapter, you may be looking to read more broadly and establish a new rhythm. If you don't know how to do that, I'll suggest a simple rule of thumb: for every recently published book you read (like the one you're reading now), read an old classic. Do that for the next year; go back and forth—old and new—until you get a feel for the ancient way. Get acquainted with the big Christian story that covers the centuries and spans the continents.

As you apprentice yourself to the saints of old, their way of being will open up a new field of options for you. Their examples will encourage you. Their sacrifices will provoke you. And, to the extent that their lives looked like Jesus', his way will make even more of a home in you.

## EIGHT

# The Wisdom of Rest

For he knows our frame; he
remembers that we are dust.

—Psalm 103:14 ESV

L ife has a way of depleting us. From the time of the
first family's rebellion in Genesis 3 to this very day,
the fertile ground we have been given to work is littered
with thorns and thistles. Often it can feel like an unre-
lenting tug-of-war between the ground and us. From
the beginning we see that the human heart and the soil
have an almost symbiotic connection: as our hearts were

hardened in the garden of Eden, so was the ground. The address of the Creator God to Adam after he had rebelled rings with a note of familiarity:

> "By the sweat of your face
>> you shall eat bread,
> till you return to the ground,
>> for out of it you were taken;
> for you are dust,
>> and to dust you shall return."
>
> (Gen. 3:19 ESV)

The drops of perspiration fall from our faces as the wheels of work grind on. Life is hard. We know the struggle. We fall into bed every night with an awareness of all we *didn't* get done that will be waiting for us in the morning.

> "Cursed is the ground because of you;
>> in pain you shall eat of it all the days of your life."
>
> (Gen. 3:17 ESV)

But while life as superintendents of God's creation is often hard, it is not just hard. It is also suffused with holiness. Louder than the endless list of things calling for our attention, the seventh day calls to us.

By the seventh day God had finished the work he had
been doing; so on the seventh day he rested [*shabbat*]
from all his work. Then God blessed the seventh day
and made it holy, because on it he rested [*shabbat*] from
all the work of creating that he had done. (Gen. 2:2–3)

For millennia, the meaning of the Sabbath has occupied the hearts and minds of the rabbis. Much time and
creative energy have been spent ruminating and endless
books have been written on the right way to observe this
day. Some rabbis recommended wearing special garments
in honor of the Sabbath, which would be a way of wel-
coming the day that rises above all other days. Other
schools of rabbis taught that a person should walk with
an easy gait on the Sabbath compared to their more severe
weekday stride to signify their entrance into the holiness
of time. The cup of wine would be lifted, and prayers of
sanctification (*Kiddush*) and blessing (*Havdalah*) would
be prayed at the beginning and ending of the Sabbath day.
After the people had received God's rest, and as the day
was coming to a close, the rabbi would stand up and pray:

Glorious greatness and a crown of salvation, even the
day of rest and holiness, Thou hast given unto Thy
people—Abraham was glad, Isaac rejoiced, Jacob and
his sons rested thereon—a rest granted in love. . . .

. . . Our God and God of our fathers, accept our rest; sanctify us by thy commandments, and grant our portion in thy Law; satisfy us with thy goodness, and gladden us with thy salvation; purify our hearts to serve thee in truth; and in thy love and favor, O Lord our God, let us inherit thy holy Sabbath.[1]

The rabbis were serious about embodying the rest of God in a weary world. But for all that has been said through the centuries, one of the clearest articulations of the Sabbath has come to us in our own time by Rabbi Abraham Joshua Heschel. Born in 1907 in Warsaw, Poland, Heschel spent his formative years watching the rise of Nazi Germany. What he observed was, in his mind, just another iteration of the human attempt to construct the Tower of Babel. In his stunning little book *The Sabbath*, Heschel writes:

Technical civilization is man's conquest of *space*. . . . Yet to have more does not mean to be more. The power we attain in the world of *space* terminates abruptly at the borderline of *time*. But time is the heart of existence.[2] (emphasis mine)

Heschel also notes that "while the deities of other peoples were associated with places or things, the God of Israel was the God of *events*: the Redeemer from slavery, the Revealer of the Torah, manifesting Himself in the events of history rather than in things or places."[3] God is the God over time and invites all creatures made in his image to enter into the cadence of the cosmos.

In the creation account, the first six days of work are spoken of as overwhelmingly "good" (*tov*). Six times in the first chapter of the Bible, we're told that "God saw that it was good" (Gen. 1:4, 10, 12, 18, 21, 25). And at the end of the sixth day, when God created male and female in his image and bestowed upon them the authority to "have dominion" (Gen. 1:26 ESV) over his world, there is a great crescendo in the text: "And God saw everything that he had made, and behold, it was *very good*" (Gen. 1:31 ESV, emphasis mine). The Hebrew here is *tov me'od*, which means "muchness, abundance, exceedingly."[4] God looked at the creation and saw abundant *muchness*, endless possibility, and a world teeming with life, which gave him much happiness.

But as good as the first six days were, the seventh day—the Sabbath day—was altogether different. "Then God blessed the seventh day and made it *holy* [*qadash*]" (Gen. 2:3, emphasis mine). The Sabbath is a consecrated day of *otherness*, a sacred space of sanctity, the day in which the world is to be swept back into the leisurely holiness of God's very self. At this point, we are beginning to discern the compellingly beautiful Hebraic understanding of time: the *goodness* is in the work, but the *holiness* is in the rest. And without rest, the work that was meant to be good becomes a curse. Indeed, the six days of work can be good *only if* the one day of Sabbath is kept holy.

Rabbi Heschel claims that God built into the infrastructure of the cosmos a place into which we image-bearing humans can retreat. It is a realm of holiness, a place of protection where our well-being is preserved. It is a place to "be still, and know that [he is] God" (Ps. 46:10) and to remember that we are not. And while the Sabbath is a sort of invisible edifice, those who regularly run into it are saved.

The Hebrew word for "rest," *menuha*, conceptualizes the creation of an absence, a stillness and peace. In his reading of the creation story, Heschel asks a question and then answers it: "After the six days of creation—what did the universe still lack? *Menuha*." Rest was the final piece of the puzzle. "Came the Sabbath, came *menuha*, and the universe was complete."[5]

Only those who give themselves over to the absence can discover the fullness of the Presence. Those who sit in the emptiness of the Sabbath day begin to overflow with God's fullness into the other six days. Far from being an arbitrary command, just another hoop to jump through, the Sabbath introduces us to the graciousness of God, for it is the day where we do absolutely nothing and discover that we are still deeply loved.

## The Idolization of Vacation

The ancient Egyptian pharaohs who worked the people of God to death may be long dead, but they are still very much alive in the hearts of Westerners. Their whips and cudgels lash and crack at our psyches, and their slave-driving tactics taunt us with that ancient cry: "More bricks, less straw!" (see Ex. 5:6–9). That old, oppressive spirit lives on and animates so many of us to this day, having fully convinced us that we are only worth what we produce. In some strange genealogy of financial systems, Pharaoh's production economy begot America's production economy, or it is at least its distant relative. To hold on to the lie that "we are what we produce" means to let go of the Sabbath gift.

Somewhere deep in our bones, we know that we are breaking the command to rest. And we know that in breaking it, we are actually ourselves being broken. To feel better about our disobedience to the fourth commandment, many of us have replaced the institution of Sabbath with the recently constructed cultural idol of vacation. Now, I don't think vacations are intrinsically bad, so give me a minute here to explain. We find ourselves drowning of exhaustion, but we think, *Oh, thank God! A life raft*—a vacation—as it is tossed to us. For a brief moment, we catch our breaths. We enjoy the momentary sensation of not floundering, before our life raft is stripped from us and we're right back into a long stretch of Sabbathless existence. We distract ourselves and keep afloat by daydreaming about our next vacation nine months from now.

We are a vacationing society (for those who can afford it), living from hit to recreational hit without ever entering into rest. Vacations can be great, as long as we understand what they are for and what they can and cannot provide. Vacations are a time to make memories with family and friends, but they can never get us back to and keep us in a healthy spot. Vacations don't heal us; they entertain us. Vacations are for occasional recreation. Sabbath is for weekly restoration. Only the Sabbath has the healing touch. Asking a vacation to get us back to a place of rest is like hoping a binge diet will restore us to a place of health. But God is calling us into holiness, and if we don't regularly pause from our daily toil, deep rest will evade us.

It's interesting to me that there are no records of vacations in Scripture. Part of that could be because most people wouldn't have had the financial means to take one. But I also wonder if it's because the Jews lived so well that they didn't need vacations. When you get tucked away into the palace of Sabbath restoration, when you are hidden in the architecture of holiness on a weekly basis, you don't have to run away to the distant lands of cheap amusement.

Don't get me wrong. I'm not arguing that we do away with vacations, only that we keep them from becoming a cheap substitute for the weekly Sabbath rest that God has made available.

## The Startling Inefficiency of God?

God is rarely ever in a hurry and usually acts as if he's got all the time in the world. But we live in a society enamored with efficiency. Books such as *The 4-Hour Workweek* and *Smarter, Faster, Better* have become bestsellers because we want to crack the efficiency code. That's fine by me. I am not advocating for a life of sloppy indolence; I am advocating for a life of Sabbath composure. We have to realize that the divine calculus of Sabbath rest does not compute in the world in which we live.

It would be easy to read the Gospels and wonder why Jesus was not in more of a hurry. The bewildered and the blind, the lepers and the lame, the hungry and the homeless seem to be everywhere. The needs of his people were endless. The Jewish people as a whole were living under the brutal domination of the occupying Roman army. It must have felt like a double cruelty to be brought back from centuries of Assyrian, Babylonian, and Persian exile only to be living as strangers in their own land, the very land God had promised to their father Abraham. The taunts of the enemies were everywhere. So, when Jesus showed up announcing the good news of God's kingdom and claiming himself to be "the Way" into that kingdom, you can imagine how that would have stirred the people's expectations of him. He also often delivered in ways that filled his people with hope. Compassion moved him to heal, to restore, to set the lonely into families.

Luke tells us what this did to galvanize the region:

> The news about him spread all the more, so that crowds of people came to hear him and to be healed of their sicknesses. (Luke 5:15)

But in the very next verse, he gives us a clue that the way of Jesus was often going to disappoint the people:

> But Jesus often withdrew to lonely places and prayed. (v. 16)

What is the Son of God doing withdrawing? He walked right past opportunities that most of us would jump at. He got away to pray. He lingered at the table with friends. He took naps in the back of the boat while the storm raged. He went on hikes, disappearing into groves of olive trees where only his Father could see him. He was in no hurry to get to Lazarus's side, even though Lazarus was in his deathbed. Jesus was so late that Lazarus's flesh had grown foul and fetid, and Mary and Martha let him hear about it. But we should have known Jesus would be like this. The fact that it took him thirty years to launch his public ministry tells us that efficiency was not God's top priority. Had it been, Jesus would have been cranking out miracles on the playground as a child. Instead, he waited till the wedding in Cana of Galilee, and even then, he was reticent.

Having been one with the Father from eternity past, Jesus moved at the pace of the divine life. He showed us that God is not in a hurry. Jesus *is* the Sabbath composure of God leisurely walking the streets of our frenetic towns. Upon further observation, it seems that his habit of withdrawing to lonely places to pray made it so that when he appeared, he was overflowing with fullness. Indeed, what often looks like efficiency is really just emptiness of spirit. We have been running too fast for too long. But Jesus refused this kind of existence.

Jesus lived out of the fullness, and he invites us into that same kind of life:

"Come to me, all you who are weary and burdened, and I will give you rest. Take my yoke upon you and learn from me, for I am gentle and humble in heart, and you will find rest for your souls. For my yoke is easy and my burden is light." (Matt. 11:28–30)

## "Be Excessively Gentle with Yourself"

Not long ago, I was in a particularly intense stretch of life and work. I was leading staff meetings and preaching every week. I had been asked to officiate two very heartbreaking funerals for folks in my congregation who died unexpectedly. Death can rarely be planned for and is always emotionally expensive, leaving one feeling spent, or even bankrupt, for weeks and months. On top of it all, my family and I had sold our house and were living for several months in a temporary housing situation while waiting to move into our next one. We weren't in a crisis by any means, but we were exhausted.

Mercifully, my friend, Pete Greig, showed up from England to spend a few days with me and to preach at our church. We've been friends for two decades, so he knows me, and I trust him. I didn't have to pretend to be put together with him. One day, we went to Café Velo for a cortado, and I told him about the last couple of months.

It was a stream-of-consciousness rant, but he listened graciously and intently, kindly receiving the force of my negative energy. His friendship felt like the dawning of a Sabbath that I desperately needed.

Once I had unburdened myself of all that I had been carrying, Pete sat for a moment in sympathetic silence. And then he said five words I'll never forget: "Be excessively gentle with yourself."[6] He went on: "Take a few days off. You and Lisa should take more walks." He suggested I sleep in one morning and get off the hamster wheel of endless activity. His words, like the words of Elizabeth to her cousin Mary (Luke 1:41–45), caused hope to do a cartwheel in my spirit.

So much of life is spent around people who are deeply vexed, who desperately need to borrow strength from us. Like one of the first six days of creation, this work of being available is "good" work. But there are days when our souls begin to fray at the seams, and we are frightened by it. There are days when all our endless activity catches up with us, and we're on the brink of collapse. Those are the days you need to "be excessively gentle with yourself."

Go where nobody knows you. Give yourself the time to grieve. Give yourself space to tip over into loneliness, so that when you finally get there, you can find the God who longs to be your truest friend.

## Learning to Be Unhurried

Being with Eugene Peterson was like being ushered into an alternate realm with an entirely different relationship to time. The cadence of his life moved to the beat of heaven. There wasn't a frenetic bone in his body.

But let me clear up something here: so often when people talk about living a life of rest, they seem only to be able to present a picture of a life of perpetual leisure, of vacations and regular golf trips and spa weekends. They don't talk about what it looks like to live a rested life while still experiencing the warp and woof of daily work. They have to *stop* all work and go away from it completely to find rest. They are describing the tricky threshold, where rest devolves into sloppy indolence. Vacations and golf trips and relaxing weekends can all be wonderful in themselves, but when they are your only way to live a rested life, something is out of whack.

Eugene Peterson's restfulness was entirely different. He had figured out how to live a rested life while still being thoroughly engaged in his work. Whereas some folks are pining for lives of perpetual leisure, Eugene lived in and operated from a *purposeful leisureliness*. And from it came a body of work that stands toe-to-toe with any accomplished author of his generation. His productivity was born out of an unhurried leisureliness.

Just what does this purposeful leisureliness look like? What are some of the concrete practices that substantiate it? I saw Eugene live it as he rose early in the morning to come face-to-face with God. Some people jump out of bed in the morning and allow themselves to be caught up in the rat race. Eugene, though, started his day by stopping; he engaged the world by retreating. The first ninety or so minutes of his day were spent in his study, slowly meditating on the Scriptures and quietly pouring himself out in prayer. His decades of silent awe in the presence of the Lord resulted in the steeling of his soul.

I saw Eugene live this purposeful leisureliness as he left his work desk to engage in daily exercise. He went on walks through the woods surrounding his home. He kayaked, canoed, and swam in Flathead Lake. Earlier in life, he told me he ran some twenty marathons. I saw his leisureliness on full display as he worked in the herb garden with his wife Jan. I experienced his leisureliness through his letter writing (most of his communication happened by snail mail till the very end of his life). He knew that all good writing comes from wholesome humans with invigorated imaginations, and his daily exercise got the blood flowing and kept his mind sharp. He didn't see it as an hour less of writing in his day but as an investment in his writing.

Eugene directed me to that crucial scene in Herman Melville's *Moby-Dick*. Captain Ahab is leading his crew in their quest to spear the great white whale. The ship is chasing it and all the sailors are astir, but one man is sitting in the boat, calm and untroubled. He is the harpooner, and about him Melville writes: "To insure the greatest efficiency in the dart, the harpooners of this world must start to their feet out of idleness, and not from out of toil."[7]

Eugene Peterson was a harpooner, and his words were like darts straight to the human heart. That is because he refused to be in a hurry, because he had learned how to live a rested life in the midst of the swirl.

## Withered Lives Made Whole

In Matthew 12, we find an instructive little story. It would be easy to miss as it takes up only six verses. One Sabbath day, Jesus is walking through the grain fields to the synagogue. It was time for church. When he gets there, the text tells us that a man with a shriveled hand is worshiping among the festive throng. My imagination races as I read the text: Was the man off in the corner? Was he considered unclean? Did people assume his malady was some sort of judgment from God? Were they staring at him? The Pharisees obviously noticed him, making an example of him in church: "Looking for a reason to bring charges against Jesus, they asked him, 'Is it lawful to heal on the Sabbath?'" (Matt. 12:10).

The ancient Jews had taken seriously the call to Sabbath rest and, therefore, had fortified the day with all manner of rules to keep people from violating it. But these rules were getting in the way of doing good works. Jesus, knowing they were missing the point of the Sabbath, made a massive claim: "'For the Son of Man is Lord of the Sabbath.' . . . Then Jesus said to the man, 'Stretch out your hand.' So he stretched it out and it was completely restored, just as sound as the other" (Matt. 12:8, 13). In just a few sentences, Jesus let the world know that the Sabbath does not exist so a rigid rule can be followed. It exists so our withered lives can be made whole.

Therefore, take care of yourselves, my friends. Know when to be gentle with yourself. There is rest for you: for your *bodies* as well as for your *souls*. For if you're going to be a gift to the world, you're going to have to rest. Wisdom is found in knowing when to draw away so that you can step back in with something to give.

Receive his gift. Follow Jesus—the Lord of the Sabbath—into his Sabbath rest.

# NINE

# The Wisdom of Holy Lament

My God, my God, why have you forsaken me?

—Psalm 22:1

O ne of my friends was in crisis. He was walking through the valley of the shadow. A small group of friends gathered and yielded the floor to him. We were in no hurry. Tears began to stream down his face. "This has easily been the most difficult year of my life," he said. We felt the weight of his words. We did not try to positively "spin" the moment. No one tried to manipulate the moment by reminding him of all he had to be grateful for. We let our friend speak like one of Israel's psalmists, who cried out in pain and exhaustion. After an appropriate amount of silence had settled over us, this came out of me: "You have permission to live the most difficult days of your life in the safety of our presence."

What I told him is a pretty good description of what a Christian community can be when things are working as they should: a safe place. A Christian community should be a place that grants permission to feel the loss, permission to grieve, permission to be where we are, and permission to tap into the pathos of the God who feels. The easiest verse in the Bible to memorize is the shortest one in the whole book, made up of only two words: "Jesus wept" (John 11:35). It's found in the story of the tragic death of Jesus' close friend Lazarus. Jesus arrived and was standing on the outskirts of the village with Lazarus's sisters, Mary and Martha. They were surely wailing and reeling and feeling caught up in the maelstrom of human emotions. From what we read, Jesus didn't try to cheer them up. He felt their sadness and wept.

But people don't always feel they have been given that permission, the permission that Jesus afforded Mary and Martha, the permission that my friends and I gave to our dear friend walking through the most difficult year of his life. And, because of it, we have so many emotionally stunted Christians walking around like robots. They carry a Bible in their hands but have only a faint glimmer of light in their eyes. I think there are at least three factors in play that keep people from telling the truth about their situation, even as the pressure of life is enclosing around them: two are cultural, and the other is theological.

First, we Westerners live in a moment of great strength. We have robust armies and booming economies. We have more computer technology in the smartphones tucked into our back pockets than the first spaceship that carried a man to the moon. And, collectively, we have longer life expectancies than at any other time in history. The evidence is all around us. To present anything other than strength would be letting out the secret: *In this world of plenty, if things are not going my way, then I must be the problem.*

Second, we live in an age that has largely forgotten how much time and effort it takes to be emotionally healthy. Any discerning human being in the developed world must know that a war is actively being waged for our time and attention. Workaholism is praised in our society. It is a sign of the "new virtue." Parents are invited—maybe even expected—to keep their kids so busy with sports and music and extracurricular activities that a home-cooked meal shared around the table feels like a small victory.

We no longer know how to jump off the hamster wheel of activity long enough to check in on ourselves and other people. We are in a constant state of busyness.

But what about the third factor—the *theological* factor—that keeps us bottled up? There are some folks who understand faith to be a rugged shake-off-your-feelings-and-move-on type of thing. Some people have been taught that faith means ignoring the painful realities of life in favor of a grit-your-teeth positivity. I know this version of faith all too well because I grew up in Tulsa, Oklahoma, which is one of the primary greenhouses for what many Pentecostal charismatics call "word of faith" theology.

"Word of faith" theology found its footing in the late 1800s, and it was based on a handful of key scriptures:

And by His stripes *we are healed.* (Isa. 53:5 NKJV, emphasis mine)

Beloved, I wish above all things that thou mayest *prosper* and *be in health*, even as thy *soul prospereth*. (3 John v. 2 KJV, emphasis mine)

The thief comes only to steal and kill and destroy; I have come that they may have life, and *have it to the full.* (John 10:10, emphasis mine)

*Death and life are in the power of the tongue:* and they
that love it shall eat the fruit thereof. (Prov. 18:21 KJV,
emphasis mine)

In this particular theological calculus, a certain formula begins to emerge. If you add up all these flagship
scriptures, here is what you are left with:

1. We have to understand what "the finished work of
   Jesus" on the cross purchased for believers, which
   can be appropriated and experienced *right now* in
   *all its fullness.*
2. We have to understand that God always wants us
   to prosper *in every area of our lives.*
3. We have to understand just how important it is
   to maintain a "positive confession" so we don't
   mess up the formula and talk our way out of God's
   blessings.

It's a theological tightrope. But if you can walk it,
you're told, the full complement of the benefits of salvation will be yours *on this side of eternity*: physical health,
financial prosperity, and a long life of imperturbable peace
and emotional stability. The whole package is available if
you just "have enough faith." The believer doesn't have
to wait in eschatological hope for that day when Christ

returns to set things right. The believer doesn't have to wait for *anything*, in fact, because their lives can be firing on all cylinders right here and right now.

There are at least two problems with this theological approach: (1) it can be realized only by small pockets of people living in the first-world West and a few other wealthy regions around the globe; and (2) if you're a believer who happens to be experiencing a season of difficulty, you're left feeling a great deal of shame. Indeed, the soft implication is that if you're *not* experiencing victory in every area of your life, there must be some "hidden sin" that you are carrying. (Few pastors will go so far as to make that accusation explicit.)

Lest you think I'm on a mission to malign my "word of faith" brothers and sisters, please hear me: I'm not. That is my theological "home country," and I cherish my upbringing. The church services I grew up in were alive and lively. We believed anything could happen at any moment. I still carry with me the instincts that were formed in me in those days that God is good and intends good for us, and that our words are powerful and must be guarded. I still look for the work of the Spirit to break in at any moment, and I'll always have a love for laying hands on the sick. (I'll discuss this later in the book.)

But if we're not careful, one of the implicit messages communicated will be: If you struggle at all, it's your fault.

If you're scared, where is your faith? If you're wrestling with grief, what's wrong with you? And if you think this message is only prevalent among "word of faith" believers, it's not. We're *all* in danger of falling for this fallacy.

## Lament: An Invitation to Tell the Truth

How in the world did we ever get here? All it takes is opening up the Old Testament to see that the people of Israel were not afraid to share their feelings with Yahweh. The book of Psalms introduces us to an official—and very unique—literary genre called "the laments." In fact, almost two-thirds of the Psalms are classified as one form of lament or another. These people were not afraid to name their difficult realities. They were not afraid to shoot straight with God and say hard things to him.

> With my voice I cry out to the LORD. . . .
> *I pour out my complaint before him.*
>
> (Ps. 142:1–2 ESV, emphasis mine)

> *How long,* O LORD? Will you forget me forever?
> *How long* will you hide your face from me?
> *How long* must I take counsel in my soul

and have sorrow in my heart all the day?
*How long* shall my enemy be exalted over me?
Consider and answer me, O Lord my God.

(Ps. 13:1–3 ESV, emphasis mine)

In one of Israel's national laments, the people came at God with an outright accusation:

*You* have rejected us and disgraced us
　and have not gone out with our armies.
*You* have made us turn back from the foe,
　and those who hate us have gotten spoil.
*You* have made us like sheep for slaughter
　and have scattered us among the nations.
*You* have sold your people for a trifle,
　demanding no high price for them.
*You* have made us the taunt of our neighbors,
　the derision and scorn of those around us.
*You* have made us a byword among the nations,
　a laughingstock among the peoples.
. . .
*All this has come upon us,*
　*though we have not forgotten you,*
　*and we have not been false to your covenant.*
*Our heart has not turned back,*
　*nor have our steps departed from your way,*

yet *you* have broken us in the place of jackals
and covered us with the shadow of death.

. . .

*Awake!* Why are you sleeping, O Lord?
*Rouse yourself!* Do not reject us forever!

(Ps. 44:9–14, 17–19, 23 ESV, emphasis mine)

These words, pulsing with fury and exasperation, are enough to make the average believer blush. We know what proper decorum looks like when it comes to being in the presence of presidents and prime ministers, and we would never consider using such speech. But here it is in the Bible. Here it is given to us by the ones fastened in the yoke with God.

Lament is the act of speaking up, of maintaining a voice, of taking up our side in the divine-human covenant interaction. Indeed, it cannot rightly be called a "covenant" if the stronger party (God) doesn't allow space for the weaker party (us) to speak up. That sort of arrangement would only be tyranny. But because God is a covenanting God, we see him giving us, the weaker party, space to voice our concerns and complaints.

Jesus himself is the icon of what faithfulness before the Father looks like, and when we turn to the end of the Gospels, we read about his travail in the Garden of Gethsemane. He takes the disciples with him to pray, and in a moment of great honesty, he tells them, "My soul is deeply grieved, to the point of death; remain here and keep watch with Me" (Matt. 26:38 NASB). Matthew's account goes on:

> And He went a little beyond them [in the garden], and *fell on His face and prayed*, saying, "My Father, if it is possible, let this cup pass from Me; yet not as I will, but as You will." (v. 39 NASB, emphasis mine)

In another gospel account, Luke gives us a glimpse of Jesus in Gethsemane through the lens of a physician: "And being in anguish, he prayed more earnestly, *and his sweat was like drops of blood falling to the ground*" (Luke 22:44, emphasis mine). It's possible that Dr. Luke was using hyperbole to state the obvious, namely, that the weight of the world was collapsing in on Jesus. But it's also possible that he was describing an occurrence of hematidrosis, a medical phenomenon caused by severe mental distress, where tiny capillaries rupture near the sweat glands, mixing blood and sweat that then spill out of the pores.[1] Such knowledge lies beyond the scope of our knowing, but of this we can be certain: before having his body crushed, Jesus was being crushed to the very depths of his being.

Jesus was then betrayed by Judas, arrested and beaten by the guards, and his fragile and naked body nailed to a cross. Matthew takes us up to the hill called Golgotha and tells us important details:

> From noon until three in the afternoon darkness came over all the land. About three in the afternoon Jesus cried out in a loud voice, *"Eli, Eli, lema sabachthani?* [My God, my God, why have you forsaken me?]" (Matt. 27:45–46)

As he was being suffocated to death in front of the gawking crowd, Jesus prayed a prayer that is taken directly from Psalm 22:1: "My God, my God, why have you forsaken me?" Walter Brueggemann suggests that Psalm 22 is about "the desperate attempt to sustain praise when one's world is falling apart."[2] *Praise?* How is a prayer like that considered praise? It's considered praise because in the very worst moment of his life, Jesus addressed not the Roman authorities, the Jewish leaders, Judas who sold him for thirty pieces of silver, or his closest friends. Jesus addressed *his Father.* He lifted his voice to heaven, for he knew that was where his help comes from (Ps. 121:1).

And the church has been praying those words ever since. During Lent, the forty days of fasting and soul preparation that get us ready for the joys of Easter, the church leans heavily on Psalm 22 as a model for maintaining faithfulness during severe testing. The use of this psalm suggests that the nature of prayer is found in our openness and vulnerability before the Lord. According to Brueggemann, "unless you're living in the framework of a covenant, you don't dare get angry."[3]

As we pay attention to Jesus' words on the cross, we discover that God wants truthful communication from us, not some watered-down, reserved, dispassionate speech in sterilized language. Jesus, the Word of God, wants our words to bleed, to have a pulse, to be *alive*. Lament prayers are ancient Israel's tools of choice for keeping the divine-human dialogue alive and vibrant.

## The Costly Loss of Lament

What happens when we jettison lament as a necessary part of our dialogue with God? In his article "The Costly Loss of Lament," Dr. Brueggemann answers:

> One loss that results from the absence of lament is the loss *of genuine covenant interaction* because the second party to the covenant (the petitioner) has become voiceless or has a voice that is permitted to speak only praise and doxology. Where lament is absent, covenant comes into being only as a celebration of joy and well-being. Or in political categories, the greater party

is surrounded by subjects who are always "yes men and women" from whom "never is heard a discouraging word." Since such a celebrative, consenting silence does not square with reality, covenant minus lament is finally a practice of denial, cover-up, and pretense.[4]

When we shut out our negative emotions, something in us dies. And the dynamic *imago Dei* that is the bedrock of our existence suffers damage from the cover-up. Even the most pagan therapists and counselors would agree. But sadly, too many Christians have mistaken lament as faith*less*ness, when it is actually a sign of faith*ful*ness. To speak up to God is to believe that he cares, that he longs to hear from us, and that he's willing to take in the full spectrum of our emotions. To speak up to God is to believe that he has the power to act and to change situations that have been intractably stuck for so long. To speak up to God is to believe that his goodness will be the final act in the long drama of our lives.

Lament must not be lost in the life of the church. If Israel cried "How long, O Lord?" over and over again, we, too, must raise our "How long?" to God. As we do, the church becomes what it was always meant to be: a safe haven for all the wounded and the disenfranchised among us, and a place where they can recover their hearts after having recovered their voices.

Because I spent so many years around believers who understood avoidance to be a form of reverence, I have had to slowly practice my way into using truthful speech with God. Over the last few years, I have learned to pray the Psalter's laments, and even written my own in times of trial. I have taken these "How long, O Lord?" prayers (Ps. 13) and prayed them for the starving refugees wandering through the Yemeni wilderness. I have called on the Father and prayed "Do not hide your face from" the diseased children in the slums of India (Pss. 27:9, 102:2). I have prayed "Awake, Lord! Why do you sleep?" (Ps. 44:23) as I thought through the homeless single parents struggling through dead-end jobs and sleeping in their cars in the dark shadows of our cities.

As a pastor, I go into hospital rooms and darkly lit funeral homes and teach people that their cries do not scare God. What we see in the Old Testament, and ultimately in the life of Jesus himself, is that the saints have historically been so secure in their God that they were able to share their most troubling feelings with him.

## Faith in *What*?

Many have mischaracterized our time as an age of unbelief, of opposition to faith. But that is wrong. The explosion of the self-help genre over the last hundred years ought to be our first clue that we live in an age of deep spiritual longing, of endless searching, among a people hoping to find the transcendent. We talk about the higher power somewhere out there and Mother Nature right here among us; our athletes thank the man upstairs after a great performance. There is a collective desire to tap into the positive energy we believe is coursing through the cosmos. Spiritual gurus and mystic instructors can be found everywhere, and their YouTube channels have more subscribers than the churches have members. People are looking for help and for hope, for answers and for miracles. People are dying to get caught up into a larger story, into something with ultimate meaning. And all these hopes are easily filed under the word *God*. But when "God" means everything, it ends up meaning nothing.

It is into this muddled morass of hopes and longings that the Bible falls into our laps. The writers of the sacred texts do not call us to a general faith that "things are going to work out in the end." They do not call us to a vague belief in some sort of inevitable cosmic justice. Faith, for the biblical writers, is not an abstraction. They call us to faith *in God*, and through their storytelling, the word *God* is invested with specific meaning. We begin to discern his character; we begin to see what he is like through his dealings with his people Israel. And the call of the New Testament becomes dramatically more specific, calling us to entrust the entirety of our lives to this man, Jesus Christ of Nazareth.

Lutheran theologian Robert Jenson has written the most helpful sentence that I have come across on identifying just exactly who God is: "God is whoever raised Jesus from the dead, having before raised Israel from Egypt."[5] Or, as the writer of Hebrews put it, "[Jesus] is the radiance of God's glory and the exact representation of his being" (Heb. 1:3). The focal point of the biblical witnesses, and the hinge upon which the two Testaments turn, is Jesus. And the call of biblical faith is to deny ourselves, take up our crosses, and chase him wherever he may go (Matt. 10:38, 16:24; Mark 8:34; Luke 9:23, 14:27).

But why Jesus? Why not follow one of the many other good teachers and spiritual gurus out there? Because Jesus, we're told, is the only one in whom God and humanity have been irrevocably joined together. When the 318 bishops gathered at the Council of Nicaea in AD 325, this is precisely what they hammered out: Jesus is the restored communion of heaven and earth; he is the coming together of God and man; and he is the Second Adam, who, by his obedience unto death, rescued us from the death brought on by our own disobedience. As the drafters of the Nicene Creed put it, Jesus is,

God from God, Light from Light, true God from true God; begotten not made, of one being with the Father. Through Him all things were made. For us and for our salvation He came down from heaven. By the power of the Holy Spirit He became incarnate from the Virgin Mary and was made man.

Being the only Son of the Father, he makes sonship and daughterhood available to all who put their faith in him. But because Jesus' call to exclusively follow him was a threat to the Roman authorities and the temple hierarchy, they falsely accused him, mocked and beat him, pierced and crucified him. It looked as if Jesus' story had come to a sad end until, on the third day, he was raised to life by his Father and vindicated as the world's true Lord. He ascended into heaven and "sat down at the right hand of the Majesty in heaven" (Heb. 1:3), where he remains inexhaustibly alive, and the church reminds itself every time it recites the Nicene Creed that "he will come again in glory to judge the living and the dead, and his kingdom will have no end."

So maybe the question isn't "*What* is the object of our faith?" but "*Who* is the subject of our faith?" And his name is Jesus. Though he experienced the depths of despair and ached with every feeling of godforsaken abandonment, his story would not stay there. He rose on high and reigns forevermore. This is why the church resolutely calls us to put our faith *in Jesus*, and not in our own ability to "stay positive" or to "keep our heads up." It is precisely here, with the suffering Messiah, that all the suffering and confused and depressed saints find hope.

It is here with Jesus that every despondent disciple learns to pray the psalms of lament. It is here with Jesus that the saints find the guts to share their most troubling feelings with God.

## TEN

# The Wisdom of an Active Life

And they heard the sound of the Lord God
*walking in the garden* in the cool of the day.
—Genesis 3:8 ESV, emphasis mine

**M**ost people living today in the developed world are living through an almost imperceptible crisis. I will call it the "crisis of inactivity." The acclaimed psychiatrist Dr. John Ratey can tell us all about it, having spent much of his professional life researching the correlation between the performance of the brain and the activity of the body. In his book *Spark: The Revolutionary New Science of Exercise and the Brain*, he writes:

> The sedentary character of modern life is a disruption of our nature, and it poses one of the biggest threats to our continued survival. Evidence of this is everywhere: 65 percent of our nation's adults are overweight or obese, and 10 percent of the population has type 2 diabetes, a preventable and ruinous disease that stems from inactivity and poor nutrition. Once an affliction almost exclusively of the middle-aged, it's now becoming an epidemic among children. We're literally killing ourselves, and it's a problem throughout the developed world, not merely a province of the supersize lifestyle in the United States. What's even more disturbing, and what virtually no one recognizes, is that inactivity is killing our brains too—physically shriveling them.[1]

He cites several studies that show how brains housed inside inactive bodies experience measurable *physiological* changes. When we stop using our bodies, and exercise falls by the wayside, our brains actually shrink over time. Dr. Ratey cautions that too many of us think the brain and the body are "separate entities," completely autonomous from each other, which is simply untrue. Researchers have discovered that when we vigorously use our bodies, proteins are released "through the bloodstream and into the brain, where they play pivotal roles in the mechanisms of our highest thought processes."[2] Exercise results in decreased anxiety, stress, and depression; and in increased cognitive function and "synaptic plasticity," which aids learning and strengthens memory.[3]

For most of human history, people have had to live as hunter-gatherers. The prayer that Jesus taught us to pray— "Give us each day our daily bread" (Luke 11:3)—would not have been heard by them as some sort of feel-good poetic flourish. In an agrarian society, people woke up every day ready to work for their daily bread. Whereas people once engaged in the strenuous physical labor of harvesting their food, we now simply push a button to roll down our window at the drive-through and food magically appears. A sedentary slide. Whereas people once could go only as far as their feet could carry them, we now hop in a car or ride the train. A sedentary slide. And with the large portions of food that are served in the average American restaurant, our bodies are being overtaken by calories we are no longer burning.

I'm not trying to romanticize "the good old days" and present the rugged life of the hunter-gatherer as something attractive. It's not. Living in a technologically advanced world can be absolutely wonderful in so many ways. But still, we may be the first society in human history in which a large portion of the populace has the *option* to live a sedentary life. To complicate things, the industrial revolution that swept through Europe and the United States from around 1760 to 1840 forever changed the way work is done. Previous to this revolution, men and women worked primarily with their hands. But today, machines do most of the work, which means fewer workers are needed, and the ones who *are* working are no longer exerting the same physical labor. There has been a fundamental shift in the way we use our bodies.

In the middle of World War II, Dorothy Sayers argued that this lack of physical exertion was leading to great societal ills. First, there was a lack of *purpose*. She spoke about factory workers "whose work consists of endlessly and monotonously pushing a pin into a slot."[4] They used to be able to take pride in having something to show for their backbreaking work, but now they go home feeling bested and made obsolete by the machines they stand next to all day long. Second, Sayers observed what she thought to be an uptick in *sexual promiscuity*: "The mournful and medical aspect of twentieth-century pornography and promiscuity strongly suggests that we have reached one of these periods of spiritual depression, where people go to bed [with each other] because they have nothing better to do."[5]

In essence, Sayers was suggesting that the daily physical exertion was good for instilling a sense of purpose, and it was good for preserving morality and strengthening the bonds of marital fidelity. People who are tired at the end of the workday are less likely to stay out carousing and sleeping around. The downfall of King David came at just such a moment. When he should have been off at war, doing what kings do, he stayed back in his palace and, in his boredom, ended up spying on and taking advantage of Bathsheba, wife of one of his soldiers (2 Sam. 11). According to Sayers, because the button-pushing workers of her day were *not* tired, they were finding other ways to use their bodies. Finally, she says, "It is . . . a failure to discharge pent-up creative energy into daily work that drives a civilization into that bored and promiscuous sexuality, which derives *not from excess of vitality*, but from lack of something better to do"[6] (emphasis mine). In short, the sexual revolution we have experienced in the last fifty years might just be, in part, the natural consequence of our physical inactivity.

Mahatma Gandhi put it quite simply: "It is a tragedy of the first magnitude that millions of people have ceased to use their hands as hands. . . . If the craze for machinery methods continues, it is highly likely that a time will come when we shall be so incapacitated and weak that we shall begin to curse ourselves for having forgotten the use of the living machines given to us by God."[7] Something critical is lost when we stop actively using our bodies.[8]

## The God Who Is Active

From the very first page of Scripture, we are introduced to a God who is active. A quick glance at the superabundance of verbs in Genesis 1 says it all: God *created* the heavens and the earth (v. 1). God *separated* the light from the dark (v. 4). God *made* the vault above the earth (v. 7). God *made* the two great lights—the sun and the moon—and *set* them into place (vv. 16–17). God *created* the sea creatures and the winged birds, and *blessed* them (vv. 20–22). God *made* the wild animals (v. 25). And, in a sort of trinitarian anticipation of the God whom Jesus would reveal to us, Genesis 1:27 tells us that God *created. . . .* God *created. . . .* God *created* humankind in his own image. Then, to top it all off, God *blessed* them (v. 28). After the workweek we read about in Genesis 1 and 2, God must have loved his Sabbath rest.

But we know what comes after the good days of creation from reading Genesis 3. After Adam and Eve had buckled under the weight of the Serpent's seduction, we read: "They heard the sound of the LORD God *walking in the garden* in the cool of the day" (Gen. 3:8 ESV, emphasis mine). The text tells us that God moves. God is not some static deity, some sheer force of power that exists "somewhere out there" in the great unknown. God, we're told, goes on evening walks. And with what we know of our triune God—Father, Son, and Holy Spirit—we can say with great theological precision that he is intrinsically *active*. God is perpetual life. The Father is always affirming the Son: "This is my Son, whom I love" (Matt. 3:17); the Son is always giving himself over to the Father: "Into your hands I commit my spirit" (Luke 23:46); and the Spirit of the Father-Son love is always racing out into all the earth to draw humanity into this love. This back-and-forth of the trinitarian life must mean that the world—and our work in it—was always meant to be generative and vibrant and, well, *active*.

If we need any more evidence of this truth, we're told that when Jesus first bursts onto the scene in the Gospels, we find him *walking* the shores of Galilee to the Jordan River to be baptized by John the Baptist (Matt. 3:13). God in the flesh is out on another one of those evening strolls. Using his body. Getting his blood flowing. *Active*. The four gospel writers tell stories of him walking from village to village, going only where his feet could carry him. We hear about him climbing up into the hills to pray. (Where I'm from in Colorado, people call that hiking.) We're told that he grew up in Joseph's house, the house of a carpenter, which means he would have surely worked with his hands, building homes for families to live in and crafting tables for families to break bread around. Physical work. And he was best friends with a ragtag group of fishermen. I've been on some fishing boats, and fishing for a living—gathering, spearing, netting, angling, trapping, and hauling—can be backbreaking work.

Jesus, being God, shows us what God is like. In him we see that God is the God who lives on the go. The call Jesus put out to the disciples was clear: "Come, *follow me*" (Matt. 4:19, emphasis mine). This is not passive language. This is not a call to a life of lethargy. And the call still rings out today: "Follow me."

## We Have Already Been Warned

Christian thinkers throughout the centuries have categorized all human waywardness into a list known as the seven deadly sins. When the enemy is having his way with us, we are afflicted by pride, greed, lust, envy, wrath, gluttony, and sloth.

The word *sloth* comes from the Latin word *acedia*, which is a combination of the negative prefix "a" and the Greek noun *kēdos*, meaning "care, concern, or grief."[9] The word describes someone who just doesn't care, someone who has stopped being concerned about work that they *should* be engaged in. It would not be possible for me to overstate how concerned the church was with the sin of *acedia*. It was so threatening that the fourth-century monk Evagrius of Pontus spoke of "the demon of *acedia* . . . [as] the one that causes the most serious trouble of all."[10] When sloth seeps into our spiritual bloodstream and our bodily routine, we find ourselves sinking into listlessness and indolence. We stop feeling. We stop caring. Vigor wanes and passion recedes. We become like the frightened person in Jesus' parable of the talents:

> "Master, I knew you to be a hard man, reaping where you did not sow, and gathering where you scattered no seed, so I was afraid, and I went and hid your talent in the ground. Here, you have what is yours." But his master answered him, "You wicked and *slothful* servant!" (Matt. 25:24–26 ESV, emphasis mine)

The wise servants in this story kept moving, whereas the wicked servant had been seduced into sloth.

Growing up, my parents read the Bible to my sisters and me. We would read through the Proverbs each month, and I was always fascinated by this portion of Proverbs 26:

> Loafers say, "It's dangerous out there!
> Tigers are prowling the streets!"

and then pull the covers back over their heads.

. . .

A shiftless sluggard puts his fork in the pie,
  but is too lazy to lift it to his mouth.

(vv. 13, 15 THE MESSAGE)

*Acedia* is a sort of chronic and irrational indolence that takes over our lives. Motivation comes to a grinding halt. And the church fathers and great spiritual writers of the past didn't just see it as *physical* laziness but as *soul* purposelessness. It is love gone lame. It is the collapsing of the spirit that "dries up the bones" (Prov. 17:22). There are people who maintain jobs and have deep pockets that cannot finally satisfy their bankrupt souls.

As Jesus said, "Man shall not live on bread alone" (Matt. 4:4). These startling words from Jesus suggest that we humans are not primarily hungry for food but for unbroken contact with the God who speaks, and by whose word we are brought back to life. We are hungry for *purpose*, for a reason to live. We were made with the sacred fire coursing through our veins, fire that burns up slothful slumber and makes us jump out of bed in the morning. The fire that was always meant to take us out beyond ourselves for the sake of the world.

In Dante's *Divine Comedy*, Purgatory is the training ground out of the depths of the Inferno and back up to the heights of Paradise, where the slothful find themselves constantly running at top speed. It's the only way for them to shake out of it—to reverse the curse of *acedia*. In the first centuries of Christian history, to fend off this threatening demon of sloth, the ancient Christians practiced a sometimes extreme form of asceticism. They engaged in spiritual disciplines such as fasting and prayer, they lived lives of self-denial and almost dangerous frugality, and many of them moved away from the comforts of home to live in the rugged Egyptian desert. Saint Isaac of Syria said that "ease and idleness are the destruction of the soul and they can injure her more than demons."[11] The world we live in today runs on the twin principles of ease and idleness. Asceticism, which we can think of as chosen discomfort that helps keep our edge and put us face-to-face with Jesus, became the primary way for monks to stay awake in a sleepy world. Paul, in his first letter to the Corinthians, wrote, "I strike a blow to my body and make it my slave" (1 Cor. 9:27).

Many of us have been rendered inert in our spirits. Many of us are trapped in the snare of sloth. For many of us, life has grown cold because the sacred fire is flickering. The only answer for some of us is to push and challenge ourselves in a way that we haven't in years, which, I think, will help shake us out of our slumber.

## Growing Old Well

Some people are students of wine, and some are students of history; some people are students of politics, while others have devoted themselves to gardening. But I am a student of old people. I am always scanning the horizon of humanity for that look of life in the eyes of the elderly. And when I find it, I am quick to pull that person aside to ask them questions. Where are you from? What was your family upbringing like? How did you spend your working years? What were your greatest challenges? What has brought you the most joy in life?

I am particularly interested in chasing the common threads shared among the people who age gracefully. How did they get toward the end of their lives with that noticeable vigor and quick joy? In all my years of questing, I say, without a shred of exaggeration, that all of them mentioned engaging in regular routines of exercise. Now let me be clear: none of these people were caught up in our present-day fascination with having washboard abs and bikini bodies. None of them were gym rats. None of them ever mentioned their regular adherence to a grueling "leg day." In fact, my generation is really the first generation to have thought about the gym as a destination. My grandfather lived a vibrant life of eighty-five years without ever having a gym membership. He just walked and worked and repaired tractors and threw around hay bales. He turned wrenches and bent down into the soil to repair irrigation lines. He kept moving.

Over the years of talking with and paying attention to my friend Eugene Peterson, who himself lived a vibrant eighty-five years, I discovered much the same thing. He ran marathons and hiked around the Rocky Mountains and swam regularly in the frigid Flathead Lake. (I've gone for several swims with him in the Flathead, and I can tell you that either you'll die of hypothermia or it'll be the most invigorating and productive workday of your life!)

Eugene wrote extensively about a long period of time he called "the badlands," regular stretches of despair and loneliness brought on by vocational pressures to be a successful pastor put on him by his denominational leaders. What did he do to stay sane during those long stretches? He hit the trails, pushed his body to the limits, and, in doing so, found sanity in the presence of the Holy Spirit. Dr. Ratey's research in *Spark* shows the incredible creative benefits that come with daily exercise, and Eugene's own life was a case in point. I know he ran at least twenty marathons, and I count thirty-five of his books on my shelf.

My wife and I both grew up playing competitive sports, and we played into college; she was a brilliant and school-record-setting volleyball player, and I was a very average Division 1 basketball player. (She played all four years of college, and I played just one.) We had early-morning practices and two-a-day conditioning sessions in the heat of summer. We had team weight-lifting sessions before practice and late-night study halls after practice. Our strength and conditioning coaches had us on regimented diets and monitored our nutritional intake. The lessons we learned, the failures we experienced, the successes we had, and the memories we made can never be taken away from us. And as we look back on those formative years, we realize that we are still riding the wave of what we learned then: the grit and discipline and stick-to-itiveness that life demands from all of us. After those twenty-plus years of regular physical activity, routines and patterns have been set that, if continually observed, will serve us into the latter years of our lives.

And so we keep moving. It turns out that what we all learned in science class is true: a body in motion stays in motion.

## Responding to the Crisis: Charting the Way Forward

It's clear that we are living in a crisis of inactivity due to the dramatic changes in our work patterns. We all know how easy it is to sink into slothfulness in a society that values ease and comfort. But we also see that to be made in the image of God is to be made to *move*. So how should we respond to this crisis? We should be creative with how we build activity into our lives.

When someone asks me for a meeting, about half the time I'll respond with "bring your walking shoes." We'll go outside and walk around the church building, or we'll meet up on a hiking trail. Something about walking opens up the heart and clears the head, making honesty and vulnerability more natural. Sometimes we speak more candidly shoulder to shoulder on a trail than we do seated face-to-face across a desk.

Some of you are healthy enough to take up running. If you haven't run in years, don't worry about it. Go find a high school track near you and slowly jog your first hundred meters. Take a break, and when you're ready, do it again. Spend twenty minutes getting your blood flowing. And do it twice a week. Some of you who are unable to run can walk and stretch and make simple changes, such as eating smaller portions of food, that will start to pay off right away. Some of you who, like my friend Dave from church, are paralyzed and limited in what you can do, still have ways to increase your heartrate. Dave comes to church in his wheelchair and wheels around, pumping his arms incessantly. He turns up worship music on his smartphone, zips around our lobby for thirty minutes, and prays while doing so. He tells me he wouldn't be able to stay sane without these exercises. He's one of the most vibrant guys I know.

All of us are in different stages and different scenarios, but most of us can do *something* to increase our activity. Most of us can make simple but life-altering changes. Most of us can get moving enough to where we find a new tipping point into a more vibrant life. What I've learned is that these kinds of changes become a sort of self-perpetuating loop of fresh life. Newton's laws of motion taught us that an object in motion tends to stay in motion, and an object at rest tends to stay at rest, unless the object is acted upon by an outside force. If you're already in motion, stay in motion. If you're at rest, let this chapter serve as an outside force that's acting upon you.

Welsh poet Dylan Thomas, in maybe his most memorable poem, wrote: "Do not go gentle into that good night," and in another refrain said, "Rage, rage against the dying of the light."[12] It's likely that he was writing the poem for his father, who was ill at the time and would die soon after it was published. Maybe Dylan saw his father making peace with his impending death when he thought his dad had another good stretch in him, and so was urging his father to do whatever he could to maintain hope.

We cannot be entirely sure what the circumstances were that caused him to pen these words, but they can be our words. We live in a world that is devolving into idleness and comfort, but we can fight against it.

# ELEVEN

# Developing a Theology of the Laying on of Hands

Then the LORD God formed a man from the dust
of the ground and breathed into his nostrils the
breath of life, and the man became a living being.

—Genesis 2:7

**L**ife is created by touch.

When things are working according to God's creational design, human life arises from the mutual exchange of intimate *touch*. Two bodies are joined together as lovers find delight in each other, and their delight, which comes from God, is incarnational. Their love becomes *flesh* in that precious little baby swaddled, lying in the bassinet. The writer of Genesis was right: the two (parents) shall become one (baby).[1]

No longer constrained within the tight walls of mommy's womb, that little baby begins to feel her way about the new world, working to find her bearings. Her eyesight in the beginning is obscured. Like the blind man after Jesus' first touch, the other people walking around in the background over mommy's shoulder look more like trees. But that's just fine because mom can be *felt*. Being held closely by loving parents is the baby's first experience of the good life. The connection between mother and child is forged and cemented as the child holds on for dear life— the gentle clasping of mom's finger, faces meeting in the soft kiss on the cheek. The baby's very life is found by living at her mother's breast. A holy embrace. As the baby becomes a toddler, his sense of identity is nurtured by means of these holy touches.[2] Bedtime stories end with dad running his fingers through his hair, playfully squeezing his nose, and kissing his head before turning out the light.

In this chapter, I want to suggest that it is by the proper laying on of hands that we first find the world to be a safe and congenial place. But as soon as we start school, we retrace the steps of young King David, for every play-ground has a bully. Our local Goliath quickly teaches us that the laying on of hands is *not always* a good thing. As we progress through school, we take the language that for many years has been *in our ears*, and begin to deepen our understanding by getting it *into our hands*. Our horren-dous penmanship fills booklets and binders as evidence of our journey of discovery. We don't just learn the alphabet by singing a song. No, we trace and sketch on paper, erase our mistakes, and then try again. Then one day, we look up to find that we know how to get around our corner of the world just fine.

But as much as life begins with, and is nurtured by, a holy touch, the very worst moments of our lives are often caused by an unholy touch. A child who has been abused by a parent or a priest or a coach knows this all too well. A spouse, having to file domestic violence charges against the one with whom they exchanged vows, knows the sting of love that has been lost. War itself is a perversion of the gift of touch writ large. And like communicable diseases, touch *transfers*. Just as insecurity and fear can be trans-ferred through the improper laying on of hands, so can the kingdom of God, the joy of the Lord, and the life of faith be transferred by the laying on of holy hands. Touch, we discover, can go either way. It can be a way to heal and a way to harm.

## Woven into the Fabric of Creation

In the beginning of the endlessly fascinating first pages of the Bible, creation commences because God is talkative. "And God *said*, 'Let there be light,' and there was light" (Gen. 1:3, emphasis mine). The creative Word that then went racing out into the chaos hasn't stopped ever since, resurrecting things into holy order. Out of the primordial nothingness comes a distinctly physical, full-bodied creation. We have rocks and trees, skies and seas, and birds that are raising their carols in honor of their Creator. The garden we call home is full of herbs and herbivores having their way with the place.

As we thumb through the Bible and turn to the second page, we discover that the Creator God brought the human family into existence by matching up his *words*—literally, his "breath"—with the work of his *hands*. We're told that Israel's God, far from being above manual labor, rolled up his sleeves and got to work. Humanity has long had trouble conceiving of a divine being who willingly condescends into active participation with his creatures. We think, if God is anything like our presidents and heads of state, he couldn't possibly have time to get tangled up in the trivialities of daily life. We think God must be somewhere "out there," tied up in the complexities of running the machine.

But Scripture remains insistent: God went to work. "Then the LORD God *formed* a man from the dust of the ground" (Gen. 2:7, emphasis mine). He grabbed a handful of dirt and, in the way that only God can, fashioned it into a clump of flesh. Hebrew *Yatsar*, meaning "formed," is a word our forebears used to describe the work of the Creator in those inaugurating moments. It is the same word they would later use to describe a potter crafting a vessel out of clay, or a craftsman carving an image out of a block of wood.

In those early days, God knew there was no creature yet suitable for the man, so he went back to work, saying, "'It is not good for the man to be alone. I will *make* a helper suitable for him.' . . . So the LORD God caused the man to fall into a deep sleep; and while he was sleeping, he took one of the man's ribs and then . . . *made* a woman from the rib he had taken out of the man, and he brought her to the man" (Gen. 2:18–22, emphasis mine). Like the fashioning of a beautiful city, or a heavenly chamber, or a strong tower, God "made" (*banah*) the woman.

The great Craftsman is hands-on, always delighting in his work. The creation is physical, and the holiness of touch is woven into its fabric.

## When I Look Throughout Scripture . . .

When I look throughout Scripture, I find it everywhere.

Genesis 32:22–32 tells the story of how Jacob got his

new name, Israel: by *wrestling* with the angel of the Lord.
So fierce was the struggle that the angel said, "Let me go."
Now, I know this must seem so obvious as to border the
absurd, but one doesn't wrestle without affixing one's hands
on the other. Touch is required. And just how locked-in do
you have to be for an angel to want to tap out? But Jacob
refused to let go, saying, "I will not let you go unless you
bless me" (v. 26). For this, he was given a new name:

> "Your name will no longer be Jacob, but Israel, *because
> you have struggled with God* . . . and have overcome."
> (v. 28, emphasis mine)

It makes all the sense in the world that many years later,
Israel, knowing the power of touch, of holy embrace,
called his grandsons to him as he was dying so he could
lay his hands on them (Gen. 48).

As God's work of salvation grinds on through the exodus and up to the edge of the promised land, we find the
Israelites preparing for the death of the old man Moses,
Israel's great leader and lawgiver. What would these people
do? These people who didn't know themselves apart from
this man's steadying influence? Without a replacement,
these wilderness-wandering people would sink into a
quicksand pit of chaos. But God had identified the succes-
sor, and Moses had worked to raise him up. Joshua was

his name, and over time, he would learn to be "strong and very courageous" (Josh. 1:7). But courage is never accidental, and good leaders don't just happen:

> Joshua son of Nun was full of the spirit of wisdom, *because Moses had laid his hands on him.* (Deut. 34:9 NRSV, emphasis mine)

In this act, something happened to Joshua that was invisible to the naked eye. Something was *given* to him, bestowed upon him. He became more than he was on his own. Though on the outside he looked like the same old Joshua, a mysterious well had been drilled within him that opened up to deep aquifers of spiritual riches. A grace, a gifting, a calling, a special dispensation, call it whatever you like, had been unlocked and released in him that would propel him into the future as Israel's new leader.

Fast-forward into the New Testament, and Acts 9 tells us the story of Saul, the great persecutor of the church. On the road to Damascus (Syria), where he was going to round up more Christ-followers for persecution and almost certain death, the radiantly risen Jesus confronted him. He stopped Saul in his tracks and blinded him. What would Saul do? Where would he go? While stranded in a house, awaiting God's deliverance, a God-fearing man named Ananias showed up:

And Ananias went his way and entered the house; *and laying his hands on him* he said, "Brother Saul, the Lord Jesus, who appeared to you on the road as you came, has sent me that you may receive your sight and be filled with the Holy Spirit." (Acts 9:17 NKJV, emphasis mine)

The list goes on and on: Jesus commissioned his followers to lay their hands on the sick (Mark 16:17–18); Paul laid his hands on Timothy (1 Tim. 4:14; 2 Tim. 1:6–7); the elders laid their hands on the sick (James 5:14); and the writer of Hebrews called this practice one of "the elementary teachings about Christ" (Heb. 6:1–2). The ancient Christian practice of the laying on of hands is both central and undeniable. Its power is something that cannot be empirically measured or accounted for in tidy Excel spreadsheets. Nevertheless, it's true, it's real, and it carries those who have been blessed by it. But have we, today, moved beyond it?

## The Moment We Find Ourselves In

We find ourselves in a moment of great social dislocation. Throughout the ages, families have lived together. It wasn't unusual to have three or four generations sleeping under the same roof, spending their days together working the land. Agrarian societies were built on the expectation that children would grow up apprenticing under their elders, learning the family business before taking it over one day. As land was passed down through the generations, great care was given to it. Roots in a community went deep. And families lived this way because they *had to*. There were few other, if any, economies out there strong enough to support the single-family lifestyle we have grown accustomed to in our time. We live in a moment of a thousand options. For the first time in human history, large segments of people can *decide* where they want to live. Most of us have opportunities to whimsically explore the world. And if we don't like where we are after a few years, we can just find a new place. Retirees can pick the coast they want to live on, or they can decide to "snowbird" in warmer climates during the long winter stretches and come back home when the weather warms up. A thousand options.

And the moment we find ourselves in is a moment of cheap connections. We may have 1,500 friends on Facebook, but we haven't had a meaningful conversation in quite some time. Many of us have grown fat with connections, but we are anemic in relationships. Even our communities of faith are feeling the loss. Statisticians and pollsters everywhere will tell you as much. People who used to regularly attend church have stopped.

Instead of attending worship services *in the flesh*, many watch online. Something that was meant to be a last resort for deployed soldiers and hospitalized saints has become the first option for many. The societal move toward the virtual has gotten into the bloodstream of the church, who is herself at risk of becoming the church of the disembodied.

The church, though, has always been *of the body*. We lift up our holy hands and sing at full volume. We bow our knees at the altar and anoint the sick with oil. Worship is physical. Embodied. When Jesus called his disciples to remember him, he didn't mean in happy, transcendental thoughts on which to meditate. He gave them bread and wine, a meal. And he gave them *each other*. With his last breath on the cross, he said to his mother, Mary, and his best friend, John, "Woman, here is your son" (John 19:26). He meant: *There's a new family for you. Stay together, because you are going to need each other.*

With our social dislocation and cheap connections, we are at risk of losing the gift of physical proximity. We are at risk of losing the gift of the laying on of hands. But the church has always been the body of embodiment; the church is the means by which Jesus continues to lay his hands on us. This touch is felt as another saint stands in his place and lays their hands on us.

## When I Think About My Life . . .

My life is a compilation of moments where holy people laid hands on me. It began with my parents, and they got me off to a great start. They prayed, and they prayed, and they prayed, calling on the Lord to fulfill the plan he had mapped out for me before the world began. They would personalize Psalm 139 as they prayed over me:

> For you created [Daniel's] inmost being;
>> you knit [him] together in [his] mother's womb.
>
> . . .
>
> Your eyes saw [his] unformed body;
>> all the days ordained for [him] were written in
>>> your book
>> before one of them came to be.
>
> (vv. 13, 16)

My pastor Billy Joe Daugherty, a man of bulletproof integrity who has since entered his rest, and whom I loved dearly, would regularly come over to me and, laying his hands on my head, say: "Father, raise Daniel up to be a mighty man of God. Anoint him for service and use him for your glory." (Our church believed in this stuff.) I'm riding the wave of those prayers to this day.

On and on the prayers would wash over me as

honorable people in my life would lay their hands on me. Their names are Mark and Linda Turner, Jim and Pam King, Tom and Susan Newman, Sharon Daugherty, Artis Himes, Lance Ivey, Gyle Smith, Pete Greig, and Oral Roberts. Like a quilt of unique but complementary patterns stitched together, my life has been a bringing together of various spiritual heritages that have been imparted to me over the years.

When, as a grieving and disoriented young pastor, I met Eugene and Jan Peterson, they were in a position to receive me with some semblance of strength. On my first visit, Eugene was a vibrant seventy-seven-year-old saint who had just finished writing *Practice Resurrection: A Conversation on Growing Up in Christ*, the fifth manuscript he had written in five years. His mind was not only energized but was also energizing to me, his young interlocutor. He would rattle off exact quotations from Kierkegaard and von Balthasar, Torrance and von Hügel. To be with him was to be invigorated.

I'll never forget visiting him when he was eighty-five. Flying into that tiny Montana airport, I felt the sober seriousness one feels when visiting an aging grandparent. It was one of those trips you take because you don't know how many more of these you'll get. We spent two days walking and talking, swimming in and kayaking on Flathead Lake, and praying and reading through his library. I have always loved spending time with people in their eighties and nineties, because I know they are a treasury of experiences. So I came ready with questions.

At the end of our second day together, I asked if I could pray for Eugene and Jan. But I took it a step further, asking if I could anoint their heads with oil. There is an unmistakable significance to oil throughout Scripture. It's the way people were "set apart" as holy unto the Lord, and it signifies the "oil of gladness" for which every human being is longing. This felt like a big thing to ask, a younger person asking to anoint a sage. They were emotional as they said yes, of course, I could anoint them with oil. Toward the end of my prayer, I asked, "Father, let them hear your affirmation in the depths of their being, 'Well done, good and faithful servant.'" It was a moment I will never forget.

Eugene then got up and went to the other room. He came back carrying his own bottle of anointing oil. When he cracked that thing open, the room immediately filled with that unmistakable smell of frankincense from the Middle East. He anointed me with oil, and he and Jan prayed for me. He took the oil and made the sign of the cross on my head. He did the same on my hands. He prayed so many wonderful things (all of which I recorded and will cherish forever), but these words stood out to me: "Father, help Jan and I to take what's left with us and share it with those around us. . . . *Help us give it all away.*"

Eugene and Jan Peterson knew what Scripture tells us over and over again: something happens when the people of God pray for one another, lay hands on one another. There is a transference in the spirit, a grace unlocked that, though invisible to the naked eye, wells up into fresh strength for our long pilgrimage across planet Earth and into the kingdom that will have no end. Like Israel with his grandsons, like Moses with Joshua, like Ananias with Paul, like Paul with Timothy, and like Jesus with the children who came running up to him. For believers, the laying on of hands has always mattered, and it still matters today.

I know that many of you reading this book will have experienced pain at the hands of people you thought you could trust. A perversion of touch. I would never minimize or ask you to pretend as if it didn't happen. My heart aches for you, and I grieve for you with the grief of the Father in heaven who has only ever intended good for you, and who himself would never take advantage of you. I believe with everything in me that it's possible for the very thing that brought you great wounding—unholy and destructive touch—to be healed through the holiness of touch. Beauty from the ashes. New walls of protection can be rebuilt from the ancient ruins.

Do not be quick to ask *just anyone* to pray for you. Period. Go slow. Be wise. Guard your heart. But there are saints around you who are trustworthy, who have purity radiating from the depths of their being, who have "clean hands and a pure heart" (Ps. 24:4). There are saints who would know how to carry themselves in the presence of your pain, and who carry within them the restorative touch of our Father God.

And they, like Eugene and Jan Peterson, would find it a great delight to share that great spiritual heritage with you.

# CONCLUSION

## Where We Go from Here

Get wisdom, get understanding: forget it not;
neither decline from the words of my mouth.
Forsake her not, and she shall preserve thee:
love her, and she shall keep thee. Wisdom
is the principal thing; therefore get wisdom:
and with all thy getting get understanding.

—Proverbs 4:5–7 KJV

We have come to the end of our discussion, so it might be worthwhile to quickly summarize what we have learned and ask where we go from here. But first, understand that chasing wisdom is a pursuit that never stops. Nobody ever graduates from the course and moves on to new endeavors. Finding wisdom in God's world is a lifelong endeavor. Because life is dynamic and seasons change, because our bodies grow feeble and new challenges arise, because economies tank and job markets shift, because wars erupt and governments rise and fall, the demand for acquiring wisdom is constant.

We learned in chapter 1 that the wise are those who unapologetically ask for help. They pick up the phone and call. They take the chance. They live with a holy presumption. Like the twelve-year-old Steve Jobs, they know help is out there. They take Jesus at his word when he says, "Ask and it *will* be given to you" (Matt. 7:7, emphasis mine).

We learned in chapter 2 that there are sages and seasoned saints who have lived and logged miles and learned how life works through the school of trial and error. They are the people who are most often content to be in the background, but when asked, are willing—even *happy*—to leverage their wisdom to raise up the life of another. But they will not fight their way to the front, nor will they make their voices heard in the streets.[1] Sages wait for an invitation, and when it comes, they will help.

We learned in chapter 3 that sages aren't afraid to make us work hard for the acquisition of an unshakable life. Like Mr. Miyagi and Eugene Peterson, these figures refuse to be in a hurry. Sometimes they will make this perspective explicit by saying, "but not so fast." They also will not allow their apprentices to take shortcuts because they know that a false arrival foreshadows a false life. This insistence on the holiness of the process proves their love. As King Solomon once wrote, "Wounds from a friend can be trusted, but an enemy multiplies kisses" (Prov. 27:6).

We learned in chapter 4 that wisdom is found in getting acquainted with the book of wisdom: the Bible. Too often, we are tempted to think of "wisdom" as an assortment of philosophical abstractions and pithy quotations about God and the world, and that the "good life" can be strung together from all sorts of ways. But the saints have long believed the Bible to be *the Book*, the true repository of wisdom. So, spend a decade burying your face in Israel's wisdom literature, and see if you are the wiser for it. Lock yourself away in the practice room and learn the scales so that you'll be prepared to improvise when life happens. If you stick with it, you may even fall in love with the Book, which was always set up to introduce us to Wisdom himself: Jesus Christ. Read through the Gospels and get to know his life. Understand how he forgives, blesses, and even feeds his enemies. Study his concern for the poor and the downcast. Get caught up in the unbroken communion he shares with his Father. Pay attention to his regular disciplines, such as prayer and fasting. And let his biblical words get metabolized in you through daily prayer. Wisdom is found in a long apprenticeship to Jesus, by the Spirit and through the Word.

We learned in chapter 5 the wisdom of going to church. Too often we fail to live wisely in peacetime; that is, we live independently of the body of Christ. But Saint Jerome imagined the church as sort of an ark that carries us through the flood. We learned in chapter 6 the wisdom of a quiet life. The call of Saint Thomas à Kempis still rings out: "love to be unknown." And if the fields of obscurity were formative in Jesus' life and ministry, we ought to expect them to be formative for us too.

We learned in chapter 7 the wisdom of an old library, of "reading the dead people" in a society that loves novelty, and in chapter 8, the wisdom of living a life of rest in a world that runs on adrenaline. We learned in chapter 9 the wisdom of crying out in lament and contending for our emotional health, and in chapter 10, the wisdom of an active life. And, finally, in chapter 11, we learned of the spiritual heritage that can be passed on through the laying on of hands.

This list of practices is not meant to be exhaustive. For who alone can write an all-encompassing book on wisdom? But I do think these chapters are appropriately representative, and they are a good place to start on the journey toward acquiring a wholesome life, one that will stand the test of time.

But wisdom doesn't just live at the level of the *conceptual*. It is acquired and demonstrated through faithful *practice*. So get out there and give it a go.

# To the Old
# (or Almost Old[1])

**W**hether you know it or not, you are coming into your greatest years of strength. You will know by now that I'm not talking about *physical* strength. The joints ache, and a slower gait has been imposed on you by nature. The things you used to be able to do—skiing, mountain climbing, running half marathons, traveling— may not be as easy, and for some, they may not even be an option anymore. But in the economy of the kingdom of God, your value has experienced absolutely no diminishment at all. About the aging people of God, the psalmist says:

The righteous will flourish like a palm tree,
    they will grow like a cedar of Lebanon;
planted in the house of the LORD,
    they will flourish in the courts of our God.
*They will still bear fruit in old age,*
    they will stay fresh and green,
proclaiming, "The LORD is upright;
    he is my Rock, and there is no wickedness in him."
                      (Ps. 92:12–15, emphasis mine)

The experiences and the perspectives you have gained are something money can't buy and youth can't replicate. It just takes *time* to grow old and to see what you have seen. You stand on the precipice of realizing your greatest potential. Yet the society in which we live seems to be actively telling you either that you're not needed anymore or that you should retreat into leisure (to golf or go on a vacation), away from the life you once lived. Yes, you should enjoy these years, but your contribution shouldn't come to an end. In fact, this is your moment to bear the most fruit you've ever borne. This is the season where God intends to multiply your reach and extend the wisdom and experiences you have gained into the lives of others.

Think about it. You now have more disposable time (and for some, disposable income) than you have ever had. You have all you need to be a blessing to those who are following in your path. So here's my simple encouragement to you: be available. Assume you have something important to share, even if they are lessons you have learned through failure. Sometimes those lessons are actually the most valuable, and if you're willing to share them, the world will be the better for it.

Open your heart, and if you have one, open your home. Life happens, and hearts tend to open up around the dinner table. You will be surprised to discover just how many college students and twentysomethings long to hear a grandfatherly voice or feel a grandmotherly touch in their lives. You will be surprised to discover how many newly married couples yearn to learn from people who have walked the same road in front of them. Be an active participant in your local church and put yourself in position to bump into the young. Keep your eyes open and be willing to respond when asked. Share your story over coffee and ask them about theirs. And, as you do, just see what the Lord might do.

I beg you to live this way, and please believe me when I say that there is so much still to do in front of you. These years don't have to be years of withdrawal and diminishment. Some of the most important relationships in my life have come from people like you being willing to spend time with people like me.

God is able to make these remaining years your most fruitful years yet. And I'm praying that they will be. Amen.

# To the Young
# (or Not-Yet-Middle-Aged)

**T**here is something beautiful about being young. Soak it up. Sleep in a little over the holiday break during your high school years. If you can, galivant around the globe over the summer breaks of your college years. If you are newly married and plan to have children *someday*, enjoy the spaciousness of your life together. Take spontaneous weekend trips into the mountains. Car seats and diaper bags will be filling your back seats soon enough. King Solomon advised that young people should enjoy it while it lasts: "Remember your Creator *in the days of your youth*" (Eccl. 12:1, emphasis mine).

But in all your blissful enjoyment, please don't be stupid. You won't always be able to live the life that you are living now. The moment you're living in now is as uncomplicated a life as you will ever have. A life of greater complexity and increased responsibility is on its way. Solomon tells us to enjoy the days of our youth "before the days of trouble come and the years approach when you will say 'I find no pleasure in them'" (Eccl. 12:1). Old age is coming, and what you do with your lives and with your bodies and with your money in the days of your youth matters.

After considering and partaking in every kind of pleasure imaginable, Solomon, at the very end of the book of Ecclesiastes, got to the bleeding heart of the matter:

> Now all has been heard;
>     here is the conclusion of the matter:
> Fear God and keep his commandments,
>     for this is the duty of all mankind.
> For God will bring every deed into judgment,
>     including every hidden thing,
>     whether it is good or evil.
>
> (Eccl. 12:13–14)

Too many of you are living it up without considering what your deeds will cost, what your actions will mean for your future. You sleep around without thinking about the emotional, relational, and physical cost of such a life. You drink and drive without thinking about what that might mean for another person's life (or death), and without thinking what a DUI will mean for your future employment. You rack up a bunch of debt thinking you'll have plenty of time to recover without realizing how it will affect your credit scores and your ability to secure mortgage loans in the future.

The way you live now will have great bearing on what your life will look like later. Older folks know this stuff. Who better to lead you through the "days of your youth" than the sagacious saints who have navigated the "days of trouble" and come out on the other side with "robust sanity"?[1] But nothing in society will encourage you in their direction. You live in the days of the glorification of youth. You live among those who praise slim bodies instead of sound minds. You love pop stars and forsake old war veterans. You follow the tabloids for news of the latest celebrity marriages while missing out on the wisdom of the couple sitting in the pew next to you who have been married for fifty years. And to the extent to which you continue in this direction is the extent to which you forfeit one of God's great gifts.

Be humble, young people. Assume you don't know everything there is to know. Look around the landscape and seek out an older, wiser person you trust. Maybe they will be someone you know from church. Take them to lunch (plan on buying[2]) and come ready with a list of questions. Sometimes you'll be shocked by their profundity, and at other times, their answers will be subjective and will apply more to their unique situation than to yours. Either way, listen and take good notes. Don't argue. As they say in Oklahoma, where I'm from, "Eat the hay, spit out the sticks."

Ask them questions like, "What have you learned that I need to know?" Ask them, "What were some of your greatest challenges during your working years?" Ask them, "Is there anything you would caution me about in this stage of my life?" Ask them, "What have you learned about friendship?" And keep thinking about other great questions you may have. It's often frustrating when someone asks me for an appointment only to show up and find that they expect me to set the agenda and lead the conversation. If you request a meeting, come prepared. Thank them for their time, honor the bits of wholesomeness that you've observed in them, and let them know you want to continue to glean from them. Come with a legal pad and four or five good questions, and see where things go.

Don't play the fool. You don't always have to learn the hard way. If you'll take the time and do the work, you'll find sages along the way who can save you a lot of heartache. Make it your goal to spend the rest of your life chasing wisdom.

# Acknowledgments

**T**o my parents, David and Becky Grothe. Any decent contribution I will ever make to the world is a direct result of their faithful witness and the lives of wisdom they have lived out in front of me. They helped nurture in me a love for the Scriptures. They kept me around the saints and sages in our local church. They taught me to chase wisdom from the people living in the University Village nursing home just down the street from our church. Because of their lives, the seed of this book has been germinating in me from the days of my youth. Dad and Mom, the command to "honor thy father and mother" has been easy to obey with you as my parents.

To Larry and Linda Wakley, thank you for loving and raising up the woman who would become my wife. I am reaping where you've sown. It is because of your lives that my life is so rich. You can be assured that I praise God for you daily.

To Brady Boyd, my pastor and my friend, thank you for encouraging me to write all these years. And thank you for coming to Colorado Springs all those years ago at great cost to yourself. I didn't know it at the time, but over the years it has become clear: you were the gift that I needed. The wisdom you have imparted to me informs my daily work and will be with me the rest of my life.

To Pete Greig and Ken Costa, who invited me to speak at London's Windsor Castle in November 2017. Something happened in me that day, the intersection of *chronos* and *kairos*, and that moment catalyzed this book. I'll always thank God for your friendship and the chance you gave me that day.

To my agent, Alexander Field, who knew just what to do when all I had was an idea. Your sound guidance and clear direction gave this project a great jump right out of the blocks.

To my guys, Jon Egan, Glenn Packiam, Jeremiah Parks, Andrew Arndt, Brad Baker, Jason Jackson, Matthew Tisthammer, and Gyle Smith. You graciously endured the early drafts of this book and gave me feedback that made it much better. All these years of friendship with you has made me rich in all the right ways.

To Webster Younce, Sujin Hong, and all the incredible

artists and wordsmiths at Nelson Books, I shudder to think what this book would have been without your careful attention and patient precision. You helped me bring this book to life. May your tribe increase!

To my wife, Lisa Carol. You live the most elegant and gracious life of wisdom I have ever encountered. Beauty radiates from your being because you have lived your life before the face of God. If I have any authority to write this book, it is in large part due to the life you have allowed me to live beside you. I love you.

And to our children, Lillian Carol, Wilson James, and Wakley Daniel. Your lives are the greatest gift the Lord could have given your mother and me, and your lives are the greatest contribution we will ever make to the world. We love you, we are proud of you, and we will spend the rest of our lives making sure you know that. The world is going to need you, so chase wisdom as if your life depended on it.

# Notes

## Introduction

1. Mary Oliver, "The Summer Day," Library of Congress, https://www.loc.gov/poetry/180/133.html.
2. Mike Berardino, "Mike Tyson Explains One of His Most Famous Quotes," *Sun-Sentinel*, November 9, 2012, https://www.sun-sentinel.com/sports/fl-xpm-2012–11–09 -sfl-mike-tyson-explains-one-of-his-most-famous-quotes -20121109-story.html.

## Chapter 1: Learning to Ask for Help

1. Silicon Valley Historical Association, "Steve Jobs on Failure," October 31, 2011, https://www.youtube.com /watch?v=zkTf0LmDqKI.
2. Silicon Valley Historical Association, "Steve Jobs on Failure."
3. Silicon Valley Historical Association, "Steve Jobs on Failure."

4. Alina Tugend, "Why Is Asking for Help So Difficult?" *New York Times,* July 7, 2007, https://www.nytimes.com /2007/07/07/business/07shortcuts.html.

5. William C. Placher, ed., *Callings: Twenty Centuries of Christian Wisdom on Vocation* (Grand Rapids, MI: Wm. B. Eerdmans, 2005), Kindle loc. 910–14.

6. Herbert Spencer, *The Principles of Biology,* vol. 1 (London: Williams and Norgate, 1864), accessed April 23, 2019, https://books.google.com/books/about /The_Principles_of_Biology.html?id=Ye4GAAAAcAAJ.

## Chapter 2: Introducing the Sages

1. Eugene H. Peterson, *As Kingfishers Catch Fire: A Conversation on the Ways of God Formed by the Words of God* (Colorado Springs: WaterBrook, 2017), 165–67.

## Chapter 3: Learning to Work for Wisdom

1. Eugene's comments about large churches and the pastors who lead them might sound abrasive to you, as they did to many of my friends initially. But after ten years of interacting with Eugene, I've been able to learn more, ask questions, and give him some reports from "on the ground." I've written more about that at https://daniel grothe.wordpress.com/.

2. Greg Lukianoff and Jonathan Haidt, *The Coddling of the American Mind: How Good Intentions and Bad Ideas Are Setting Up a Generation for Failure* (New York: Penguin, 2018), 24.

3. The prayer has often been attributed to Sir Francis Drake, since there is so much seafaring language, but that is likely a spurious connection, because he lived in

the 1500s and the language is quite modern. After much searching, I've been unable to find a clear author. In any case, the prayer remains helpful for our purposes here.

4. Merriam-Webster online, s. v. "apprentice," accessed May 10, 2019, https://www.merriam-webster.com /dictionary/apprentice.

## Chapter 4: The Wisdom of Loving Scripture

1. Marilynne Robinson, *Gilead: A Novel* (London: Picador, 2004), 28.
2. Clement of Alexandria, "Chapter XVI: Scripture the Criterion by Which Truth and Heresy Are Distinguished," *The Stromata*, accessed April 29, 2019, http://www .earlychristianwritings.com/text/clement-stromata-book7.html.
3. Saint Athanasius' orations *Against the Heathen*. See Part III, especially *Doctrine of Scripture on the Subject of Part 3*, accessed July 19, 2019, https://www.ccel.org /ccel/schaff/npnf204.toc.html.
4. Quoted by William Goode in *The Divine Rule of Faith and Practice: A Defence of the Catholic Doctrine That Holy Scripture Has Been, since the Times of the Apostles, the Sole Divine Rule of Faith and Practice to the Church* (London: James Nisbet and Company, 1906), 462.

## Chapter 5: The Wisdom of Going to Church

1. Keith Green, "O Lord, You're Beautiful," accessed April 30, 2019, https://www.youtube.com/watch?v=uVgPQm06g2c.
2. "Why Americans Go (and Don't Go) to Religious Services," Pew Research Center, August 1, 2018, http:// www.pewforum.org/2018/08/01/why-americans-go-to -religious-services/.

3. Jeremy Weber, "Pew: Why Americans Go to Church or Stay Home," *Christianity Today*, August 1, 2018, https://www.christianitytoday.com/news/2018/july/church-attendance-top-reasons-go-or-stay-home-pew.html.

4. In Luke 2, we see that the temple was a home to the two elderly saints, Simeon and Anna. It is one of my great desires—and the consistent work of my hands as a pastor—to see the church function precisely in this way so that no elder among us is left bereft and lonely in their latter years.

5. Saint Jerome, "The Dialogue Against the Luciferians" in *Nicene and Post-Nicene Fathers: Second Series*, ed. Philip Schaff, trans. W. H. Fremantle, vol. 6 (Grand Rapids, MI: Christian Classics Ethereal Library, 1893), 726–55, http://www.ccel.org/ccel/schaff/npnf206.html.

6. Frederick Buechner, *Whistling in the Dark: A Doubter's Dictionary* (San Francisco: HarperOne, 1993), 93.

7. Buechner, *Whistling in the Dark*, 93.

8. Robert J. Karris, *Eating Your Way Through Luke's Gospel* (Collegeville, MN: Liturgical Press, 2006), 14.

9. I highly recommend following Ben Myers's blog. He's one of the clearest thinkers and wittiest writers out there. Ben Myers, "Why Go to Church?" *Faith and Theology* (blog), October 20, 2013, http://www.faith-theology.com/2013/10/why-go-to-church.html.

10. Simeon Zahl, "Hiding in Plain Sight: The Lost Doctrine of Sin," *Mockingbird*, October 2, 2018, http://www.mbird.com/2018/10/hiding-in-plain-sight-the-lost-doctrine-of-sin/.

11. Though my great-grandfather immigrated to the United States from Germany, my German is quite poor. But the phrase Marx used is "Die Religion . . . ist das Opium des Volkes." If you want to read his critique, see Karl Marx,

*Critique of Hegel's "Philosophy of Right,"* ed. Joseph O'Malley, trans. Annette Jolin and Joseph O'Malley (New York: Cambridge University Press, 1970).
12. Myers, "Why Go to Church?"

## Chapter 6: The Wisdom of a Quiet Life

1. David Newton, "Michael Oher Gives Negative Review to Effect 'The Blind Side' Has Had," ESPN, June 18, 2015, http://www.espn.com/nfl/story/_/id/13100161/michael-oher -carolina-panthers-says-hit-movie-blind-side-hurt-career.
2. See Banksy's graffiti at https://secure.flickr.com/photos /bitboy/246805760/sizes/o/.
3. Euan McKirdy, "Einstein's Handwritten Notes Sell for $1.8 Million," CNN, October 25, 2017, https://www .cnn.com/style/article/einstein-handwritten-notes-auction /index.html.
4. Thomas à Kempis, *The Imitation of Christ* (Wheaton, IL: Christian Classics Ethereal Library, 1949), 119, http://www .ccel.org/ccel/kempis/imitation.html.
5. Thomas, *Imitation of Christ*, 5.
6. Thomas, *Imitation of Christ*, 76.
7. Thomas, *Imitation of Christ*, 69.
8. Thomas, *Imitation of Christ*, 5.
9. Thomas, *Imitation of Christ*, 17–18.
10. For a brilliant little summary of *The Imitation of Christ*, check out *Christianity Today* at https://www.christianity today.com/history/people/innertravelers/thomas-kempis .html.
11. See the interview where Eugene talks about turning down the first invitation from Bono because of his translation work at https://www.youtube.com/watch?v=FaaIui7cESs.

12. Ronald Rolheiser, *The Shattered Lantern: Rediscovering a Felt Presence of God* (New York: Crossroad, 2005), 44.
13. Rolheiser, *Shattered Lantern*, 44.
14. Rolheiser, *Shattered Lantern*, 44.

## Chapter 7: The Wisdom of an Old Library

1. If you don't know where to start in developing a list of worthy reading material, I highly recommend Peterson's book *Take and Read: Spiritual Reading—An Annotated List* (Grand Rapids, MI: Wm. B. Eerdmans, 1996), xii.
2. Several surveys demonstrate that reading is on the decline. You can find one by the National Endowment for the Arts at https://www.arts.gov/artistic-fields/research-analysis/arts-data-profiles/arts-data-profile-10. Caleb Crain distills information from the US Department of Labor survey. Crain, "Why We Don't Read, Revisited," *New Yorker*, June 14, 2018, https://www.newyorker.com/culture/cultural-comment/why-we-dont-read-revisited.
3. Henry H. Wilmer, Lauren E. Sherman, and Jason M. Chein, "Smartphones and Cognition: A Review of Research Exploring the Links between Mobile Technology Habits and Cognitive Functioning," *Frontiers in Psychology* 8 (2017): 605, doi: 10.3389/fpsyg.2017.00605. The authors reference Bill Thornton, Alyson Faires, Maija Robbins, and Eric Rollins, "The Mere Presence of a Cell Phone May Be Distracting: Implications for Attention and Task Performance." *Social Psychology* 45, no. 6 (2014): 479–88, http://dx.doi.org/10.1027/1864–9335/a000216.
4. Wilmer et al., "Smartphones and Cognition."
5. Wilmer et al., "Smartphones and Cognition."
6. Kristen Houghton, "Internet Distraction: The Writer's Main

Dilemma," *Huffington Post*, October 6, 2016, https://www
.huffingtonpost.com/kristen-houghton/internet-distraction
-the-writers-main-dilemma_b_8248214.html.

7. Blaise Pascal, *Pensées*, trans. W. F. Trotter (Mineola, NY:
Dover Publications, 2003).

8. William Shakespeare, *The Merchant of Venice*, act 2,
scene 7, 34–36.

9. Shakespeare, *Merchant of Venice*, 2.7.34–36.

## Chapter 8: The Wisdom of Rest

1. *The Standard Prayer Book*, trans. Rev. Simeon Singer (New
York: Bloch Publishing, 1920). Through the centuries, the
rabbis have prayed various prayers. The one I've chosen
above is relatively new, only a hundred years old.

2. Abraham Joshua Heschel, *The Sabbath: Its Meaning for
Modern Man* (New York: Farrar, Straus and Giroux, 2005), 3.

3. Heschel, *Sabbath*, 7–8.

4. James Strong, *The Exhaustive Concordance of the
Bible: Showing Every Word of the Text of the Common
English Version of the Canonical Books, and Every
Occurrence of Each Word in Regular Order: Together
with a Comparative Concordance of the Authorized and
Revised Versions, Including the American Variations:
Also Brief Dictionaries of the Hebrew and Greek Words
of the Original, with References to the English Words*
(London: Hodder and Stoughton, 1894), 3966.

5. Heschel, *Sabbath*, 22.

6. From the poem "For One Who Is Exhausted" by the late
Irish poet and priest John O'Donohue. See O'Donohue,
*To Bless the Space Between Us: A Book of Blessings*
(New York: Doubleday, 2008), 126.

7. Herman Melville, *Moby-Dick; or, The Whale* (New York: Harper & Brothers, 1851).

## Chapter 9: The Wisdom of Holy Lament

1. William K. Hobart, *The Medical Language of St. Luke* (1882; repr., Grand Rapids, MI: Baker, 1954), 80–84.
2. Walter Brueggemann, *Psalmist's Cry: Scripts for Embracing Lament* (Kansas City, MO: House Studio, 2010), 68–85. I found this quote in Dr. John Goldingay's notes to an article he wrote, which he gave me in one of my seminary classes. Goldingay, "The Dynamic Cycle of Praise and Prayer in the Psalms," *Journal for the Study of the Old Testament* 6, no. 20 (1981): 85–90.
3. Brueggemann, *Psalmist's Cry.*
4. Walter Brueggemann, "The Costly Loss of Lament," *Journal for the Study of the Old Testament* 11, no. 36 (1986): 60.
5. Robert W. Jenson, *Systematic Theology: The Triune God* (New York: Oxford University Press, 1997), 1:63.

## Chapter 10: The Wisdom of an Active Life

1. John J. Ratey, *Spark: The Revolutionary New Science of Exercise and the Brain* (New York: Little, Brown and Company, 2008), 4.
2. Ratey, *Spark*, 5.
3. Ratey, *Spark*, 4, 246–47.
4. Dorothy L. Sayers, "Vocation in Work," in *A Christian Basis for the Post-War World*, ed. A. E. Baker (New York: Morehouse-Gorham, 1942), 89–99, 104–5.
5. Dorothy L. Sayers, *The Other Six Deadly Sins: An Address Given to the Public Morality Council at Caxton*

*Hall, Westminster, on October 23rd, 1941* (London: Methuen Publishing, 1943).

6. William C. Placher, *Callings: Twenty Centuries of Christian Wisdom on Vocation* (Grand Rapids, MI: Wm. B. Eerdmans, 2005), Kindle loc. 6117–18.

7. Mahatma Gandhi, *Bread Labour: [The Gospel of Work]* (India: Navajivan Publishing House, 1984).

8. I know there are those who would *love* to but are *unable* to use their bodies as a result of a traumatic injury or an illness from birth. The pain of this loss ought to stir compassion in all of us. Please know that I write this chapter in fear and trembling, and in the hope that readers who find themselves disabled will have found other creative outlets appropriate to their situation.

9. Merriam-Webster online, s. v. "acedia," accessed May 8, 2019, https://www.merriam-webster.com/dictionary/acedia.

10. Kelsey Kennedy, "Before Sloth Meant Laziness, It Was the Spiritual Sin of Acedia," Atlas Obscura, July 14, 2017, https://www.atlasobscura.com/articles/desert -fathers-sins-acedia-sloth.

11. Saint Nicholas Orthodox Church, "Gleanings from Orthodox Christian Authors and the Holy Fathers," accessed May 8, 2019, http://www.orthodox.net/gleanings /laziness.html.

12. Dylan Thomas, *The Poems of Dylan Thomas* (New York: New Directions, 2017).

## Chapter 11: Developing a Theology of the Laying on of Hands

1. "That is why a man leaves his father and mother and is united to his wife, and they become one flesh" (Gen. 2:24).

NOTES

2. For benefits of skin-to-skin contact, see Teresa Pitman, "The Importance of Skin to Skin with Baby," *Today's Parent*, May 1, 2018, https://www.todaysparent.com/baby/baby-development/skin-to-skin-with-baby/. It is also worth citing the opposite; see, for instance, the horrors of Romanian orphanages. Kirsten Weir, "The Lasting Impact of Neglect," *Monitor on Psychology* 45, no. 6 (June 2014): 36, https://www.apa.org/monitor/2014/06/neglect.aspx.

## Conclusion: Where We Go from Here

1. This is what the Spirit of the Messiah works into the people of the Messiah: "He will not cry out, nor raise His voice, nor cause His voice to be heard in the street" (Isa. 42:2 NKJV).

## Afterword: To the Old (or Almost Old)

1. Poet John D. Blase helped me think about what it means to find yourself "almost old"; that is, not old but no longer living in the land of youthful naivete, a sort of chronological no-man's-land. Check out his poem "Now That I Am Almost Old," and get your hands on anything he has written on his website at https://johnblase.com/2019/01/04/now-that-i-am-almost-old/.

## Afterword: To the Young (or Not-Yet-Middle-Aged)

1. Eugene H. Peterson, *As Kingfishers Catch Fire: A Conversation on the Ways of God Formed by the Words of God* (Colorado Springs: WaterBrook, 2017), 165–67.

2. As much as you try to argue against it, some of them will insist on paying. Regardless, give it the old college try. If they really want to foot the bill as a blessing to you, let them have the joy of giving you that gift.

# About the Author

**D**aniel Grothe is the associate senior pastor at New Life Church in Colorado Springs, Colorado. Daniel and his wife, Lisa, live on a small hobby farm outside of Colorado Springs with their three children: Lillian, Wilson, and Wakley.